Heroe
Fourth

Heroes of the Fourth Service

FRANK PEARCE

ROBERT HALE · LONDON

Photoset in North Wales by
Derek Doyle & Associates, Mold, Clwyd.
Printed in Great Britain by
St Edmundsbury Press Ltd, Bury St Edmunds, Suffolk.
Bound by WBC Book Manufacturers Limited,
Bridgend, Mid-Glamorgan.

Contents

We shall not flag or fail. We shall fight on the seas and oceans, we shall fight with growing confidence and growing strength in the air, we shall defend our island, whatever the cost may be, we shall fight on the beaches, we shall fight on the landing grounds, we shall fight in the fields and in the streets, we shall fight in the hills; we shall never surrender.

Victory at all costs, victory in spite of all terror, victory however long and hard the road may be; for without victory there is no survival.

Winston Churchill, 1940

Acknowledgements

The author acknowledges with gratitude the contributions provided by those who served in the ships mentioned and to others closely associated with the events.

S. Brown
T. Brunskill
H. Cook
R. Cornish
W. Cross
J. Dalgleish
C. Eccles
R. Esmond
J. Farminer
A.D. Franks
A. Goodenough
C. Green
J. Hardwick
R. Harrison
B. Hartman
P. Johnson
T. Jordan
R. Kelly
J. Levis

E. Liles
L. McDonald
R. Miller
T. Mortlake
P. O'Grady
C. Richards
W. Rouse
J. Savage
L. Stack
R.J. Travers
T. Underwood
A. Walker
L. Walters
H. Warham
G. Webb
A.S. Williams
R.E. Williams
E. Williamson
H. Woodward

Special thanks are due to:

Lieutenant-Commander W.H.L. Mead (dec.)
John Mock and Richard Cornish of the Naval Historical

Collectors and Research Association
William Mutimer of the SS *Harlesden*
Lieutenant-Commander J. Smith, RN (ret.) Chief Librarian
    at the Plymouth Naval History library for assistance in
    research
Lieutenant-Commander C. Broadway, RN (ret.)
The Paignton and Torquay public libraries
Public Record Office – ADM 199.2141. ERD/4393
Public Record Office – ADM 199.2139
Derek Pearce

The Churchill quotations are reproduced with permission
of Curtis Brown Ltd, London, on behalf of the Estate of Sir
Winston S. Churchill. Copyright © Winston S. Churchill.

Illustrations

Illustration Acknowledgements

By courtesy of the Trustees of the Imperial War Museum: 1–3, 7–14. John Clarkson: 5.
All other illustrations are from the author's collection.

Maps

To my wife, Joan, for her
support and contribution to research

Foreword

by Admiral of the Fleet Lord Lewin

In every war our island nation has fought, shipping has been the vital resource. Sufficient ships, adequately defended, to keep our people fed and our factories supplied, to take men and material to distant battlefields, have always been the pre-requisite of victory. There was a time when this was a self evident fact. With many hundreds of thousands employed in our shipyards, our docks, in our Royal and Merchant Navies and in our fishing fleets, there were few families that did not have maritime kindred. Travel abroad was a sea voyage, long enough to give the traveller a taste of seafaring. Britain was a maritime nation, our people aware of their dependence on the freedom of the sea, the sea was in our blood.

Today all that has changed. Most of our shipyards are derelict, our busy container ports are manned by a handful of men, all our fleets have been decimated, passengers are whisked from continent to continent in impersonal flying machines with none of the grace or character of ships. Today's British people are no longer inherently aware that our nation is still dependent on the sea for our prosperity and security: we are in danger of forgetting our maritime heritage.

The Battle of the Atlantic – misnamed, it was a battle fought in every ocean – started on the first day of war when the liner *Athenia* was sunk, and continued unabated to VJ

Day and beyond, for even when fighting had stopped in every other theatre, ships were still being sunk by wartime mines. On every single day, the men of the merchant navy were in the front line. On them, their fortitude and bravery, the whole progress of the war depended. In this book Frank Pearce describes in vivid detail just some of the epic incidents. There were many more, enough to fill many similar volumes. I hope those that read will marvel at the heroism of our merchant seamen and will be reminded of the contribution our merchant navy made to victory.

A TRIBUTE TO BRAVERY

Although the Merchant Navy has traditionally been categorized as the fourth service, following the seniority of the Royal Navy, the Army and the Royal Air Force, never can it be considered fourth to any service in terms of gallantry and courage.

This has been proved beyond all doubt in the sea battles of World War I and World War II, when, with little to defend themselves against either air or submarine attack and with no training in warfare, the men of the Merchant Navy fought their ships through against overwhelming odds or were sunk with grievous loss of life.

They never turned back. We owe a great debt of gratitude for their fortitude and heroism at a time when not only the survival of Great Britain was at stake but the existence of the British Empire hung by a thread on their loyal endeavours and unflinching sacrifice in the face of savage enemy action.

Introduction

In World War II, one of the most powerful men in German High Command was Grand Admiral Karl Doenitz, the architect and driving force behind the savage campaign waged by his U-boat commanders against Allied shipping and the Merchant Navy. His conviction that the German U-boat would be the principal weapon to bring Great Britain to her knees became an obsession. Britain was an island, dependent upon the flow of food and other supplies arriving from overseas. Once this procession of lifesaving commerce was stopped, then Britain would have to surrender or starve.

So it was that from 1939 merchant ships became the fundamental target for the dreaded submarine: an enemy beneath the sea, silent, unseen, deadly, the hunter killer. For the crews of the merchant ships who sailed the oceans, almost every voyage became a nightmare. Always there was fear, fear of what would happen if the ship should be torpedoed and one had to take to the rafts or boats, if time allowed, or worse, how quickly death would come if it meant trying to swim for it.

But the pitiless torpedo was not the only peril. In the Arctic and the Mediterranean, hordes of Nazi dive-bombers roared down out of the skies to drop high explosive bombs on the almost defenceless merchant vessels. The Royal Navy's escort ships fought magnificently in trying to defend these vulnerable prey, but, particularly in the early part of the war, so few could be provided by the Admiralty, that protection was inadequate and the losses of our trading ships soared alarmingly.

It was during these early years of the war that Admiral Doenitz's ruthless campaign to starve Britain into surrender by sinking merchant vessels faster than they could be built, bordered on reality.

The shortfall in the provision of naval escort vessels must surely hark back to the pre-war government's reluctance to rearm in the face of the inevitability of war with a mighty, armed Germany. Winston Churchill gave dire warnings of the disasters that would follow if Britain failed to do so, but he was howled down as a warmonger, and when war did break out, the incumbent Prime Minister Neville Chamberlain's policy of appeasement, though well-meaning, left this country unready for war.

It is indeed a sobering thought that in 1941 alone over 1,100 merchant ships were sunk, and even more grievous when one considers that over 32,000 of their crews were killed, 4,000 wounded and 2,000 taken prisoner during their brave endeavours to keep the convoys sailing. Undoubtedly, the survival of the United Kingdom from 1939 to 1945 rested on the men of the Merchant and Royal Navies to face up to and endure the constant crushing and devastating attacks by the enemy. The importance of the survival of Allied merchant shipping upon the oceans was never more emphasized than in Winston Churchill's letter to the President of the United States, Franklin D. Roosevelt, on 8 December 1940.

> The mortal danger to our country is the steady and increasing diminution of our sea tonnage. We can endure the shattering of our dwellings and the slaughter of our civil population by air attacks, but the decision for 1941 lies upon the sea. Unless we can establish our ability to feed this island, to import the munitions of all kinds which we need ... we may fall by the way. It is therefore in shipping and in the power to transport across the oceans, particularly the Atlantic Ocean that in 1941, the crunch of the whole war will be found.

The responsibility for the survival of the people of this island therefore, rested with the captains, officers and crews of the merchant ships, in whichever ocean they sailed. Their ships had to get through or the war would be lost. Unless the ship was already in a sinking condition they never turned back. Defying torpedoes and bombs they either fought through or were sunk.

There were many notable convoys in those five years of war, each with its terrible tragedies, its heroism and sacrifices, each writing a glorious page in British maritime history. It should have been well within the enemy's power to destroy many of these convoys, and yet, because of the courage, determination and gallantry of the men who sailed them, and despite the terrible losses sustained in the endeavours, most won through. These convoys are a fact of history. Unfortunately, the mist of time has so veiled realism, that their substance has melted into shadow. Events are a part of larger events, each sending out ripples over the ocean of years. Occasionally, some rebound to warn us that the history of war is recurrent. In the tidal war of World War II, these remarkable convoys played no small part in the deliverance of civilization and the sowing of the seeds of a new future.

Today, we live in a world of make-believe, striving to escape a reality which terrifies us, preferring mirage to the material, fiction to fact. But occasionally, as in 1914 and 1939, commonalty was abruptly brought to its feet by the intrusion of war. Millions of peace-loving people who would not normally hurt a fly, were thrown into a vast battle arena with the object of killing one another to survive. It was a time when emergencies were so frequent that they ceased to be emergencies.

But from all this, there emerged men and women who performed deeds of valour. They exhibited qualities of endurance and courage which they did not know they possessed. And it is from such episodes of history that beacons of light, though now dim and flickering, remind us that such engagements of war as the convoy battles should frequently be rekindled in our memories. Contemporary history can be dangerous material, especially when written by people who were not even born when it happened. How, for example, can they adequately present the terrors of the war at sea in World War II, when ships were under constant bombing and torpedo attack? How can they know the cold sweat of fear of being trapped below decks in a sinking ship? Or depict the anxiety that develops and expands with the knowledge that only thin steel plating lies between you and the cold black sea, through which, at any moment, a torpedo might come blasting to bring choking death in impenetrable darkness. How can they understand the strain and tension of never-ending alarms, brought about by the constant call to 'action stations', bringing nail-biting suspense, leading to exhaustion, eroding the will to endure? And if, to all this, sleep is denied, as it so often was, it is then, and only then, that having lived through and survived these hellish nightmares, that the personal, emotional and true testimony of war can be written.

Without these experiences, history is often simply a compilation of dull facts and figures, meaningless inscriptions upon tombstones for future generations to stare at and speculate upon the personal and human stories buried within. The stories here expose the realism of convoy battle with an enemy whose sole object was to destroy and kill, and promote a conscious understanding of convoy warfare of the Merchant and Royal navies. As one who lived through and survived the battles of the Atlantic and Arctic oceans in World War II, I hope to give a vivid account of their history.

1   The Miracle of the *San Demetrio*

The fact that over 32,000 men of the Merchant Navy were killed during World War II is testimony to the violence with which the battles were fought. The seas all over the globe have been the scene of many stories of courage, some never to be told, because the men who featured in them lie deep on the ocean sea beds. However, some have survived for their accounts to be recorded, and among those sagas, few can be given greater pride of place than the story of the *San Demetrio*, which by the courage of her crew and against all odds survived to again sail the seas. This is not the account of a great naval engagement, but rather the incredible story of an oil tanker, which, devastated by shells from a German capital warship, was left a blazing shambles and in imminent danger of blowing up at any moment. Yet, through the bravery of her crew, the ship was saved and brought back to the Clyde.

On 28 October 1940, the ill-fated convoy codenamed HX84, comprising thirty-seven fully laden merchant ships, formed into nine columns, left Halifax, Nova Scotia, for Great Britain, knowing well the probability of having to fight its way through the packs of U-boats which waited along the shipping routes. But, apart from the killer U-boats hiding in the depths of the sea and the ruthless dive-bombers that often roamed the skies near shore areas, there were other predators.

Loose in the north and south Atlantic, were three of Germany's pocket battleships, *Lutzow, Graf Spee* and *Admiral Scheer*. These fast, powerful warships adopted the mantle of the modern pirate, plundering every ship that crossed their path, sinking thousands of tons of shipping with the subsequent loss of life of Merchant Navy seamen. It was against these combined forces of the enemy that the Merchant Navy, escorted by units of the Royal Navy, fought to bring urgently needed supplies to Great Britain.

HX84's only escort was the armed merchant ship *Jervis Bay*; a converted passenger liner fitted with 6-inch guns, commanded by Captain E.S.F. Fegen, RN. But it was at this time that the *Admiral Scheer* of 12,000 tons, with six 11-inch guns, commanded by Captain Theodor Krancke, was in the north Atlantic, somewhere along the 44-degree north parallel, waiting to pounce on shipping coming out of Halifax. It was certainly not by coincidence that it happened to be on an interception course across the eastward bound convoy. Halifax at this period was an ideal base for German secret agents, stationed there in the guise of respectable citizens, some in responsible positions, seeking information of convoy movements from some of the thousands of seamen who passed through the port. (The author had personal experience of one of these agents seeking convoy information.) Captain Krancke was no doubt fully aware of the constitution of HX84, acquired from reliable intelligence reports, and the date of its sailing.

However, the north Atlantic is a vast ocean covering an area of roughly 15 million square miles, and to locate a convoy on passage is a complicated operation. For Krancke, it was a time of vigilance and precise decisions and calculations. Somewhere, the convoy was in the area of his search. His orders were to find and annihilate it. One or two single ships had been sighted, but Krancke had turned his vessel away without being spotted. So far Lady Luck had bestowed her favours upon him. By the skilful operation of his radar, he had avoided contact with odd ships and remained undiscovered.

Somewhere beyond the horizon, lay the crown of his endeavours, HX84, and the best chance of finding it rested with the two reconnaissance aircraft carried on his ship. Mid-morning of 5 November, one of these small seaplanes was successfully catapulted off, and soaring high, headed south-west. The pilot had been given specific instructions that once the convoy had been discovered, he was to check course and position, maintain radio silence and return immediately. Shortly after midday, the plane returned, with the news that he had found the convoy and had established that no British warships were in the vicinity. So the backcloth to the drama about to unfold was set, with the circumstances and conditions ideally suitable for Krancke's purpose.

Krancke therefore decided to attack that same day, for, if he was to achieve his purpose, it would be vital to reach the convoy long before dark. With the weather fair and the ship at full speed, Krancke headed for HX84. But the fortune which had thus far favoured him, momentarily deserted him, for in the early afternoon, the *Scheer* stumbled upon a small vessel across its path, halfway between him and the convoy. For Krancke, it was an unfortunate and troublesome interruption, for if he ignored its presence and sailed on, doubtless the ship would transmit to the convoy, warning of the battleship's presence. If he did a wide circumnavigation to avoid detection it would take *Scheer* miles off course and lose valuable time. There was therefore but one course of action. Krancke headed for the vessel and ordered it to stop. It proved to be a banana boat, the *Mopan*, and the captain quickly obeyed the order. By now Krancke's time was running out, *Mopan* would have to be eliminated. As the heavy shells from *Scheer* hit the vessel, she quickly sank and the battleship sped on its way towards the unsuspecting little fleet of merchant ships.

Within the convoy itself, hopes were running high. The first seven days had been uneventful, its passage uninterrupted. But on that evening of 5 November, when almost halfway across the Atlantic, the great seaborne world around HX84 erupted into a night of fear and terror. As *Scheer* approached, the twilight of evening was already enveloping the plodding merchant fleet. As the convoy crews peered into the fading light across the darkening waters, they could see the outlines of a large fighting ship, but barely identifiable. As it drew nearer, it could be seen that it was a battleship. But was it friend or foe?

On the bridge of the armed merchant ship *Jervis Bay*, Captain Fegen watched with increasing alarm. Surely if it was British, it would have identified itself? He at once flashed 'What ship?' Ignoring the signal, the battleship came on, reducing the range to about ten miles. But the 'bow on' silhouette against the darkening sky was difficult to analyse, vague, ambiguous. It was now about five o'clock and, with the range reduced to about eight miles, *Scheer* swept around to a broadside position, allowing all her 11-inch guns to face the target. Suddenly, white spurts of flame stabbed out from the heart of the oncoming ship, shattering the quiet of the evening, while a succession of vibratory roars like the sound of a fast-approaching express train rent the air. As screaming shells exploded among the convoy, immediately from the commodore's ship, the SS *Cornish City*, came the urgent signal, 'Scatter'.

Only *Jervis Bay* now stood between the convoy and the battleship. Without hesitation, Captain Fegen brought his ship around to face the enemy, having already ordered 'Full speed ahead' and the gun turrets to be ready to open fire, thus drawing the enemy's gunfire on to himself. For Captain Krancke, only this pestering armed merchant ship stood between him and the annihilation of the whole convoy. But the light was fading fast and he was losing time having to deal with this unforeseen resistance. Seconds later, the shells from *Scheer* were blasting into the superstructure of *Jervis Bay*. Hopelessly outgunned, Fegen knew he hadn't a chance in hell of survival against the overwhelming armament of the battleship, but by challenging the German he hoped he would gain time, that tenure of precious life, giving minutes to allow some, if not all, the convoy to escape.

It would be a sacrificial effort which, although probably

only partially successful, would undoubtedly bring tragic consequences upon himself, the crew and the ship. Fully committed, *Jervis Bay* raced on at full speed towards the enemy, reeling under the merciless barrage of shells smashing into her. Suddenly, the foredeck was ripped open in a blinding flash which momentarily left the gun crews sightless. Then, with a tremendous crash, the deck beneath the feet of the officers on the bridge catapulted them in every direction, into each other, into bone-breaking metal, into the crippling confusion of numbed minds, feelingless bodies trying to fight through the fog of stunned shock. But there were other things: eardrums blasted by the explosion, lungs gasping for air from the effect of the acrid fumes, eyes blinded by the dense black smoke. For the crew of the forward gun turret, where another shell landed, it was worse, much worse. Mercifully, most died instantly; some slowly, to watch their life blood drain away from torn arms or legs.

Moments later, more shells struck the bridge superstructure, blowing off Captain Fegen's arm. Despite the agony of his wounds, he walked to the after control but was too weak to climb into it. Although most men would have collapsed, he somehow managed to crawl back to what was left of the bridge to give further orders, but there died. With her bridge in flames, most of her officers and crew either dead or dying, and the shells from her 6-inch guns falling far short of the target, *Jervis Bay* sailed on, straight into the powerful broadsides of the *Scheer*. The armed merchant ship was now alight from stem to stern, still speeding on, still firing, trying to get within range.

In the deepening shadow of the evening, *Jervis Bay*, raced on to destruction and immortality. Still distant from the enemy, her bows deepening, she slowed, then toppled over on to her side with her masts lying along the surface of the sea. Then, bows first, she rolled over with her propellers out of water and slid forward. In the fading light, the keel gleamed evilly against the black sea and then she was gone.

Captain Fegen and his crew, in offering themselves as a certain but vain sacrifice, had upheld the most honourable and highest tradition of the men of the sea. Later he was posthumously awarded the Victoria Cross. Vain sacrifice though it may have been, *Jervis Bay*'s gallant action had compelled *Scheer*'s guns to strafe the British merchant ship with 335 shells for 22 minutes. In that period, in the gathering darkness, it had given invaluable time for some of the convoy ships to scatter, hoping to escape. *Jervis Bay* had gone, her only memorial fragments of burning debris amid a pool of great gouts of air rushing turbulently to the surface, upon a restless sea.

Frustrated by the turn of events, Krancke ordered 'Full speed ahead' and raced after the disappearing merchant ships, intent on destroying every vessel. Owing to the increased darkness, *Scheer* was now compelled to use her searchlights and fire frequent star shells to light up the ocean, and these soon found remnants of the convoy. The nearest ships now became the battleship's targets.

One of the first victims was the 10,000-ton *Beaverford* bound for Liverpool. Struck by 11-inch shells, she sank in minutes taking all her crew of seventy-seven with her. Next in line was the *Kenbane Head* and, although some managed to reach the rafts, twenty-four were killed. The next to go was the 8,000-ton *Maidean* bound for Belfast with a cargo of trucks. There was little chance for the crew to reach the lifeboats or rafts, and all ninety-one of the crew perished. Soon it was the turn of the 5,000-ton *Trewelland* with her cargo of steel. Out of her complement of thirty-nine, there were twenty-three survivors. The last ship to be sunk was the 5,000-ton *Fresno City*, with the loss of twelve of her crew. Including the later sinking of the *Vingaland*, the total death roll for convoy HX84 amounted to 251, but including the 189 who died on *Jervis Bay* that figure rose to a staggering 440.

What *Scheer* could not find by her searchlights, she found with devilishly revealing starshells, lighting up the ocean for miles. By 1930 that evening, the total number of ships afloat was thirty-three, thirty-three out of the original thirty-nine. The remaining vessels twisted and turned, plodding away at their laborious top speeds to all points of the compass, trying to avoid destruction, knowing that the battleship was somewhere behind them, perhaps among them, in the darkness, like a cat waiting to pounce.

The stark reality of the situation transcended all else. How many of them would be left by morning? It was frightening to think of the miles of sea that lay in their wake, littered with the wreckage of six fine merchant ships, oil and the many corpses of their fellow seamen. To stop to pick up survivors would be unthinkable. To do so would be to invite more disaster, another ship sunk, more men drowned. In the darkness it was impossible to see if there were any survivors, and even if there were men back there in the sea swimming, struggling, they would soon be dead from exposure in the icy Atlantic Ocean. Paralleled with these thoughts was the realization that when the news reached Britain of the tragedy of the *Jervis Bay* convoy, there would be agonizing sorrow among the near relatives of those who had died. The Government's usual announcement following similar tragedies was to confirm the sinking through radio or national newspapers with the closing announcement – 'Next of kin will be informed'. The words brought a time of crushing anxiety for those at home. Through many a window, anxious eyes watched the approach of the postman delivering mail down the street. Every rat-a-tat of the letter box set the heart pounding. Would it be the dreaded telegram bearing the words – 'The Admiralty regrets to inform you ...'

It was while *Scheer*'s guns were dispensing death and destruction among the fleeing merchant ships that its gunsights targeted on the *San Demetrio*. The tanker of some 8,000 tons could carry 12,000 tons of fuel and had a maximum speed of about twelve knots or, in terms of land speed, about fourteen miles per hour. There was nothing outstanding in her appearance, for her type was common enough, a three-island ship, tall stern-deck with funnel, bridge amidships and a built-up fo'c'sle. Between these constructional features were the two well-decks containing the tanks, in which the liquid fuel cargo was carried.

The engine-room officers and crew slept aft and the other officers amidships. In the early part of October 1940, *San Demetrio* had been secured alongside the wharf in Aruba in the Dutch West Indies taking aboard her cargo of petrol destined for Britain. This in fact was a high-grade fuel, with almost the low flash point of aviation spirit, which means it could have ignited from even a small spark and, consequently, the ship would have exploded in one mighty flash. It is necessary to establish this point, following a series of events which provided a situation verging on the miraculous.

As the battleship drew near to the doomed tanker, her skipper, Captain George Waite, having witnessed the destruction of *Jervis Bay*, realized there was no hope of escape, his ship was doomed. Anticipating the worst, and having ordered the lifeboats to be made ready, he watched the approaching enemy ship with mounting dread and anxiety. *Scheer*'s approach was casual and calculated, her forward guns moving slowly around to 'lay-on' the target — the *San Demetrio*. Seconds later, the triple 11-inch guns belched a mass of flame. As the screaming shells fell on the fated ship, the bridge superstructure was suddenly reduced into a devil's scrapyard with tongues of fire spurting in all direction. Further direct hits were scored from the second, third and fourth salvoes. The shells tore away the poop-deck and the funnel, another tore away the plates in the bow. By this time, parts of the upper deck were ablaze, while under it the 12,000 tons of petrol slopped and splashed as the decks grew hot. It was clear that at any moment this volatile cargo would explode taking everyone with it. For Captain Waite, indecision would have been fatal. He had no option than to give the order to abandon ship.

Accordingly, First Officer Mr Wilson rang the engine-room telegraph to 'Finish with engines', while below, Chief Engineer Mr Pollard having, only minutes earlier, also witnessed the destruction of *Jervis Bay*, gave the order to abandon the engine-room and then quickly got his men out on deck. The scene that met his eyes beggared description.

The bridge plate decking was torn asunder, the superstructure was crushed and crumpled like thin cardboard, while distorted plates glowed red hot.

All this time, while more shells were ripping into the ship, high explosive shells bursting overhead rained down an avalanche of shrapnel. Despite the tense and critical situation, this was not the time to panic, and the port and starboard lifeboats were carefully lowered and the forty-two crew climbed in. Unfortunately, in the bustle of clambering into the starboard boat, accidents occurred. As Mr Pollard jumped, his hand was crushed against the ship's side, considerably damaging it. As the boat was about to pull away, the last two men arrived and had to take a risky leap. Davies, the store-keeper, broke his ribs, and Boyle, the greaser, received serious internal injuries from which he later died. In the darkness of the night, intermittent moonlight showed up *San Demetrio* as a clear black silhouette. Aware that the ship might burst into flame at any moment or, worse still, explode, Captain Waite, from the port lifeboat, shouted to both crews to row away as fast as possible. Within seconds of this warning, the bridge and part of the stern erupted into a blazing inferno. Although they were now safely in the boats, the situation was extremely precarious, for they had rowed to the leeward of the ship, and if the cargo did explode it would have hurled tons of burning petrol on to the surface of the sea.

With the wind blowing towards them, this would have enveloped the boats and burned them alive. Mr Pollard's report states: 'We were then in an unhappy position, because the ship was burning furiously and we feared that she might blow up at any moment. The situation at that time was what I might describe as very dangerous.' (Extract from *San Demetrio* by Calum McNeil.) This composed, impassionate statement reflects the self-control of the man under life-threatening situations. In a frantic effort to escape, the crews of both lifeboats applied all their energies to the oars to row to windward as fast as possible. From the buckled and warped plates of the tanks, petrol was now pouring out on to

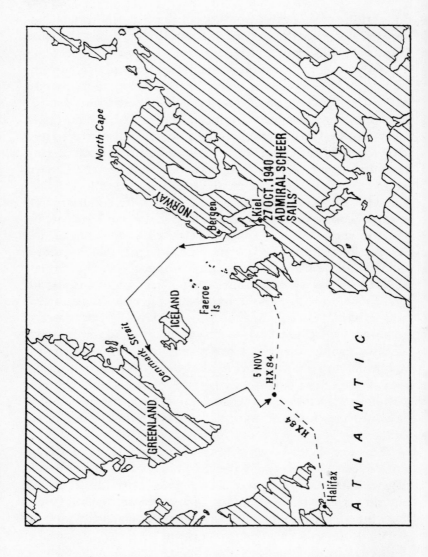

Fig. 1 Confrontation between battleship *Scheer* and *Jervis Bay*. The *San Demetrio* escapes.

the sea, creating a great pool on the surface around the ship and the boats nearby. As *Scheer* drew nearer, her penetrating searchlights lit up the whole scene. A dazzling glare that struck cruelly at smoke-seared sensitive eyeballs, transforming night into day, startlingly revealed the drama and the action upon the stage of a sea, black as the night above it. Two lifeboats entrapped within a lake of petrol; the port boat with twenty-six men and the starboard with sixteen, and close by, far too close, the *San Demetrio*, now a burning pyre assigned to her own cremation. And it was upon this lethal stage that Krancke attempted to execute one of the most inhuman acts of Nazi barbarism in the war at sea. From the decks of the battleship, a stream of tracer bullets swept across the water, sizzling and spluttering as the hot cindered shells hit the cold sea in a bid to set the lake of petrol afire and cremate the survivors in the boats.

Knowing they were sitting on a floating bomb and that at any second any one of the constant stream of tracers could ignite the sea and incinerate them, both boat crews in a frenzy of fear pulled on their oars like men possessed. The fact that the fuel did not burst into flame was against all the laws of scientific logic. The sea around the boats and around *San Demetrio* should have become a windswept roaring inferno, consuming everything in its path. Minutes later, the dazzling searchlights of *Scheer* were suddenly switched off, and the battleship moved away to find other prey.

As the boats pulled clear of the danger area, the crews laid back exhausted, but in the dark, and in their frantic efforts to escape, the two lifeboats lost contact, never to sight one another again. It was the port boat with twenty-six aboard including Captain Waite that drifted away that night, its crew later to be picked up in mid-Atlantic and taken to Newfoundland.

But the incredible story of the *San Demetrio* concerns the starboard lifeboat and its sixteen crew. In command was Second Officer John Hawkins and in addition to Chief Engineer Charles Pollard and the Third Engineer George Willey, there were two cadets, six seamen, two stewards, the bosun George Fletcher, the storekeeper, John Davies, with broken ribs and the greaser, John Boyle, suffering from internal injuries. As far as the boat was concerned, the only propulsive power was that of their own strength applied to the oars. Five minutes of hard rowing had brought them to windward of *San Demetrio* to view the flames fanned by the lifting breeze. Resting on their oars they watched their ship drift away.

As the hours passed, the wind built up to gale force with long ribbons of white streaking the water: the wave troughs deepening, their sides steepening, and with it the shrill whistle of the wind blowing along the crests. As the bows crashed down into the sea, each sickening lurch brought a shower of spray, saturating, numbing with cold indifference. Each crash into an oncoming wave brought agonizing pain to the two injured men lying in the stern. But for all of them the new strange movement in a small boat produced violent sickness. All through that night, as the heavy seas rushed on, threatening to capsize them, they were compelled to keep awake, pulling on the oars with all their might to keep the boat bows on to the rollers.

The dawn came reluctantly, lifting out of a grey gloom that barely spawned its light upon a heaving sea, revealing, as they expected, the sobering truth that they were alone. It was the end of an uncomfortable night, the beginning of an uncomfortable day, to bring only God knew what, but at this moment only a deserted horizon. Numbed with cold, plagued by seasickness, exhausted by lack of sleep, the constant demand was taking its toll. For the injured men, each jolt of the boat brought a torment of pain. But for Boyle especially, it was a nightmare of torture. Occasionally, a small trickle of blood would ooze from the corner of his mouth; bloodless lips in an ashen face told a worrying story of the haemorrhaging within. Somewhere inside that strong body was a damaged organ which needed all the skill of a surgeon's knife if he was to be saved, but, with the nearest land 1,500 miles distant, that lifesaving deliverance was purely academic.

Here in this spot of the Atlantic, in a position 52.26 degrees north, 32.34 degrees west, over 400 men had been blown to pieces, drowned or died floating in their life-jackets, their corpses strewn across the sea like a crazy pattern on a carpet of dark grey ocean. But these sort of things were the result of war, where men's lives were mere pawns on a chessboard of embattled ocean. It was happening all over the Atlantic, the Arctic, the Mediterranean and the Pacific and would go on happening for some time. That was the price that was being paid. Back home, the price of petrol would go up by one penny a gallon. But, as some of the comfortably ensconced non-participants of the war remarked with a self-pitying smile, 'It's war-time, old boy, and we all have to make some sort of sacrifice.'

Late that afternoon, a lone ship appeared over the horizon, bearing down in their direction. It was some miles away, but with the surge of hope raising their spirits and strength, the crew rowed hard to meet up with her. As they drew near, it was clear she was another abandoned tanker drifting with the wind. She was afire from stern to midships, belching clouds of black smoke. There seemed something familiar about her lines, her contours, but as most of the Eagle Line tankers were similar in design it produced no particular comment, and then, with recognition dawning, they realized it was their own ship, *San Demetrio*. So she had not blown up after all. They gazed open-mouthed.

For men adrift in an open boat in mid-Atlantic, in their condition, with only a faint hope of being picked-up, the sight of any ship drawing near was like a gift from heaven, but for it to be their own ship was something beyond their wildest dreams.

The fact that she had not blown up was a mystery, that she might still do so was a fact. Petrol still gushed from her holed tanks in the swell, flames still licked her superstructure or what was left of it, but at least she floated. One thought dominated their emotions. Dare they take the risk of trying to get aboard and put out the fires? Exultant hope was tempered with caution. In the lifting sea, she rolled heavily, awkwardly, her bows well down with green-and-white cascades of water racing across her well decks. A strange and stricken sight with her boats gone, a shattered crazily tilted centre bridge and a mangled poop-deck, buckled and twisted out of recognition by the guns of *Scheer*. A ghost ship, inelegant, lumbering in the waves, a creature of the sea without a purpose. She still had her deadly cargo, but, most important of all, she probably still had her engines, which if, and it was a dubious if, they were still operable, would save their lives.

But darkness was by now fast gathering around them, with the minutes dragging interminably by while they discussed the choice that lay before them. If they boarded the ship, it would be a gamble, with their lives as the stake. If they stayed in the boat, they risked death by drowning or more probably exposure. But as the moments passed and the darkness intensified, the chances of boarding slipped away. Again they found themselves in a lake of petrol with the realization that if their steel lifeboat, in the swell, should collide with the steel hull of the ship, it could easily produce a spark amid the swirling fumes which would hurl them into eternity. By majority, they elected to stay in the boat during the night, keeping close to the ship, and in the morning decide whether or not to board her.

But that night, the wind swung around to the north-west, bringing cold driving rain amid impenetrable darkness. At times the wind rose to gale force, lowering the temperature considerably, numbing them into a state of torpidity not far removed from that danger level of unconsciousness. Only one hope kept them alive, their *San Demetrio*, for there was now no doubt what they would do when morning came. Despite all the risk of being blown up, they would board the ship. But when the dawn light filtered across the sea, the decision had been made for them – *San Demetrio* had vanished. With the morning glow the rain cleared.

In the depths of despair, their eyes searched from horizon to horizon. Now came the regrets, the reproaches, the recriminations, the mortification of the previous day's indecision. Last night, salvation had been within their grasp, and they failed to take advantage of it. It seemed that their last chance of survival had disappeared; death from exposure seemed inevitable. The lips of one of the cadets were badly swollen and blistered, one seaman's feet had turned black and the two wounded were in great pain. Later came a flurry of showers.

As the morning wore on, the rain moderated a little and visibility improved. And then at midday, to their unmitigated joy, it cleared altogether to reveal, once again, the *San Demetrio* bearing down upon them as though appealing for their assistance. She was still on fire, still pouring out black smoke. From somewhere within them, renewed hope brought the energy and excitement they needed to reach her.

Bending their backs to the oars they soon began to draw near, and catching up with the ship, steered around to the leeward. Despite the intermittent spurts of flame and the belching smoke, to the men in the boats she looked good. They had already made up their minds. Although she might blow up at any moment, at least it would be a quick and easy death compared with the slow torture they were having to endure now. Inexorably, twice in a few hours, fortune or destiny had brought their ship to them as though pleading for a guiding hand. They would not spurn that appeal again.

At the stern, they came upon a partially destroyed rope ladder with wooden slats. Throwing wet blankets over the gunwale to prevent a spark between boat and ship, they eventually made the difficult climb to the deck, later hauling the injured men up the side of the hull. The scene that met their eyes was horrifying. The flames that licked along the upper structure had demolished the poop-deck and many of the cabins. The navigation bridge had received direct hits, and the deck of the wheel house was glowing red from the heat. In the area amidships, charts, signalling flags, wireless, the steering gear and compasses had all been destroyed. The steel plating over the main cargo-deck was buckled but more serious were the shrapnel holes through which fuel spurted with the roll of the ship. One of the shells from the battleship had exploded in the bows allowing water to enter and bring her head down. With conditions as they were, the whole situation was charged with great danger. Again the question arose, should they accept the risk and stay aboard?

But it was here, as though some mystic force was in control, that even while they were deliberating, the choice was made for them. The lifeboat which had been secured to the stern broke loose and drifted away. So now, for better or worse, they had no option, survival rested in one direction only; to extinguish the fires and eliminate the possibility of being blown up. Furthermore, to hopefully start the engines and head for home. Priority lay in extinguishing the flames, which was eventually achieved by the exhausting method of hand buckets.

When the chief engineer with three others (including the greaser John Boyle, who, despite being in an agony of pain, insisted on playing his part) reached the engine-room, they found that area under four feet of water. It had to be pumped out, and it was only by their combined skill and competence that the electricity generator was made to work, enabling them to pump the water away. Cork insulation in many parts of the ship was persistently burning, but eventually this also was brought under control. The reason why *San Demetrio* did not explode has never been explained. The fact that she did not must surely lend credence to the word 'miracle', for it defied all known scientific reasoning, and oil tankers have been known to blow up in far less perilous circumstances.

As the crew toured the ship, discovering the extent of damage and destruction, the task of applying even patch repairs seemed insurmountable. Each setback seemed to generate another setback, and when that had been overcome, some emergency arose in another part of the ship. These breakdowns occurred so frequently that, as time went by, emergencies ceased to be emergencies.

Each crisis produced first-aid solutions which had never been dreamed of in the manual of *Emergencies at Sea*. Crises, for example, where with the destruction of the bridge, the steering helm had been demolished and although there was still a little auxiliary wheel aft, flames had burned away everything but the hub and four spokes plus the wooden decking supporting it; the binnacle had dropped through two decks but was still found reasonably operable. While all these problems were being solved, the chief engineer went below to check the engines. This was another tense moment. To the astonishment of everyone, they worked perfectly, and by salvaging odd bits of undamaged wire, they succeeded in organizing a series of signal lights from the deck to the engine-room to indicate the various orders from the temporary wheelhouse.

As the little four-spoked wheel of the helm turned to head *San Demetrio* eastward, she slowly moved forward to begin her long and purposeful voyage to England and home. After all their trials and tribulations, this was a moment of triumph, of thankfulness. But that initial euphoria was moderated with caution and perhaps a deep seated anxiety, for there was a 1,500-mile voyage facing them, across an Atlantic teeming with enemy submarines. And, added to their worries, was the fact that they had no compass, no sextant to take the sun, not that there was any sun to take. Their only guide was when dawn lightened the sky to the east or the horizon became a tenuous glow to the west in the late afternoon. There was therefore nothing to aid their voyage eastward to accurately landfall the British Isles.

If they steered too far north, they would find themselves in the Arctic, too far south, in Nazi-occupied France to become prisoners in German camps for the rest of the war. Sleep was in short supply, for only a few were qualified to take a turn at the wheel. Apart from Davies and Willey, in great pain from their injuries, Mr Pollard had a dangerously swollen and useless hand, but, worst of all, John Boyle was dying. Perhaps if he had rested, there might have been a slender chance of recovery, but he had insisted on carrying on despite being in agonizing pain. Bloodshot eyes, deep sunken, hollowed cheeks told their own story. The stubborn refusal to give in, to insist on doing the job for which he was so well qualified and to perform his part in saving the ship, all this had taken a massive toll of his failing strength.

With the ship well down by the bows, the acting captain, John Hawkins, decided that to improve the situation, petrol would have to be transposed from the forward tank to one further amidships in order to raise the bows. On Saturday afternoon, under the guidance of Mr Pollard, this was successfully accomplished. On Sunday morning 10 November, John Hawkins held a short service of thanksgiving. If any one of them had previously scoffed at or had any doubt about the existence of a divine power which had controlled and guided their endeavours in the last five days, then it had been firmly dispelled. Their deliverance had been nothing short of a miracle. That same evening, John Boyle passed into a deep sleep from which he never awakened.

For the next three days they sailed on, keeping double look-outs, for by Mr Hawkins's calculations, they might see land on the third day. And indeed, late on the afternoon of the 13th, they came within sight of a coast with high cliffs atop of which were little white cottages. But where were they?

Light was now fading rapidly and they decided to keep the ship moving all that night some distance off shore. As they had no certainty as to what coastline they had arrived at, they elected to bury John Boyle before nightfall. John Hawkins' voice reading the burial service, muffled by the breeze, lent a poignancy to the simple ceremony, against the background of the stricken ship. Above them, the crazily tilted bridge and the mangled superstructure, sections of the poop-deck grotesquely askew, and elsewhere garish patches of red lead and gaping black holes. A few moments silence, then, as the board tilted, the canvas-shrouded body slid into the sea and he was gone. An unsung hero maybe but nevertheless a hero, for John Boyle had given his life to save the ship. It had been a period of tension, a nightmare scenario in which friendship and comradeship had grown into a firm and natural bond. There was nothing they could say, for the silence said everything that needed to be said. The only evidence of the true emotions of that little group of bareheaded men, was the desperate struggle to fight back the tears.

As the cold grey morning dawned, a little tug chugged its way near, and to their shouts of 'Where are we?', came the answer, 'Ireland'. So they had done it. Had achieved the impossible. They had brought this crippled tanker, with no navigational aids, 1,500 miles across the Atlantic.

Offers to accept a tow were courteously but firmly declined. Having brought the ship all this way by their own efforts they could certainly manage the last few miles to Scotland. On the morning of 16 November, the *San Demetrio* proudly navigated her way up through the Clyde, a shell-torn, dirty Red Ensign fluttering at half-mast for John Boyle, and from the after-mast a red flag warning shipping of her volatile cargo.

The report of her arrival and the heroism and achievements of her crew made the headlines of every newspaper in the country and indeed in the United States. The salvage money of over £14,000 met by the Eagle Oil and Shipping Company was distributed among the survivors. The *San Demetrio* experience was one of the most gallant episodes in British mercantile history, for out of the jaws of certain defeat they had snatched an incredible victory.

2   The Merchant Navy in the Arctic Convoys

In June 1941, German troops swarmed across its borders and attacked the Soviet Union. It was a mighty army of highly trained men, supported by thousands of tanks, armoured vehicles, guns and bomber and fighter aircraft. Such was the weight of the onslaught that the Soviet armies were driven back and back, until by October/November of that year, the invaders were only thirty miles from the city of Moscow. It was increasingly obvious to both the British Prime Minister, Winston Churchill, and to the American President, Franklin D. Roosevelt, that help would have to be given to the Soviet Union if that country were to be saved from defeat. Not that the democratic nations of the USA and Great Britain had any love for the communist-controlled Soviet Union dominated by the ruthless dictator Joseph Stalin. However, it was also clear that if Stalin's Russia were to surrender or if that country made a treaty with Hitler's Germany, then the Nazi leader would turn the whole weight and might of his armies against Great Britain. At that time we were in no position to defend ourselves, due to the ludicrous direction of the pre-war government under the premiership of Neville Chamberlain with his policy of appeasement. Between 1938 and 1939, Germany had amassed an army of some three million men and was building submarines and aircraft at an alarming rate. No country threatened her, indeed no country was in a position to threaten her. Hitler's intention therefore was obvious – world domination.

By autumn 1941, the Soviet crisis had assumed dangerous proportions. She was on the verge of collapse and needed war materials such as planes, tanks, guns etc., as quickly as possible. Roosevelt and Churchill therefore launched what became known as the 'Lend-Lease Act', whereby the USA as the arsenal of the West, would provide the greater amount of war material and Britain what she could, from the very few treasures she had. The most direct route to transport these arms was through the Arctic Ocean.

The Russian convoys started in September 1941 in convoys of British and American merchant ships loaded with war material, escorted by two or three Royal Navy warships. At the beginning of this convoy war this was all the Royal Navy could spare, because of its massive commitments in other theatres of war. From 1940 until May 1943, Germany's ruthless campaign to attack British merchant shipping in both the Atlantic and Arctic oceans expanded at an alarming rate. For the U-boat commanders it was known as the 'happy time'. Never more so than the period August 1942 to May 1943, when a total of 3,760,000 tons of Allied shipping was sent to the bottom. Merchant vessels were being sunk faster than they could be built.

At one period, 235 U-boats roamed the two oceans. With advanced techniques and improved strategy, in the spring of 1943, the Royal Navy destroyed nearly 100 of these vessels. Although Doenitz concentrated his submarine operations in the Atlantic, a considerable fleet of these killer U-boats was transferred to the Arctic in a bid to stop Allied convoys reaching north Russian ports. As the size and frequency of the convoys increased, so did Hitler's attacks with his U-boats, surface ships and aircraft based in German-occupied Norway. All this in a desperate endeavour to stop supplies reaching the Soviet armies fighting to hold back the Nazi invaders.

The battles in the Arctic lasted almost four years. One hundred vessels were sunk and over 3,000 Allied sailors killed. These battles were fought not only against the fury of the enemy but also against some of the worst weather conditions to be found anywhere in the world, demanding discipline, courage and seamanship of the highest order. And it was upon the crews of the merchant ships in convoy that the greatest burden fell, men untrained in warfare, who rose to the occasion in a magnificent display of gallantry and heroism, perhaps equalled but never surpassed in maritime history.

Between Iceland and north Russia lies one of the most turbulent areas of water in the world. Over this ocean, endless gales bringing sleet and snow whip up the sea into a succession of frightening waves, hurling themselves upon every ship in their paths. If a ship were torpedoed, the recognized survival time for a man in the water was seven minutes.

In 1941, the only possible route to Russia was through the Arctic ocean, a 2,000-mile voyage from Iceland to Murmansk and Archangel. The first of these so called PQ series of convoys set out from Iceland for Murmansk on 28 September 1941, consisting of ten ships loaded with tanks, guns, planes and ammunition. Their arrival immediately raised morale among the Soviet defenders and resistance to the enemy mounted. From then onward, regular convoys, small at first but gradually increasing in size, set out to reach north Russia.

To halt this flow of war material, Hitler increased his forces in north Norway, ready to move out to attack merchant convoy shipping. This latest move imposed an enormous strain upon the resources of the Home Fleet and as a consequence, the escort protection that could be spared for the convoys was so inadequate as to be almost negligible. To reach their destination in north Russia, the convoys had to fight their way through the narrow sea gap between north Norway and the great ice barrier. From then onward, every convoy was subjected to submarine and dive-bombing attacks, and some suffered assault by enemy warships. It is against this background in a storm-ravaged ocean, that convoys of defenceless merchant ships, escorted by units of the Royal Navy, defiantly sailed back and forth, almost on the enemy's doorstep, daring whatever form of offensive the enemy might throw at them.

This story concerns the Arctic convoy codenamed PQ13, bound for Murmansk, which left Iceland on 21 March 1942. It consisted of nineteen merchant ships escorted by the new cruiser HMS *Trinidad*, the destroyers HMS *Fury* and HMS *Eclipse* and three little minesweepers, *Silja*, *Sulla* and *Sumba*. The merchant ships carried a variety of cargo for the Russians, guns, tanks, trucks and aircraft, etc., piled high on the decks and chained down to withstand the heavy seas they would encounter. Those that showed nothing above decks were the most dangerous, carrying high explosives; if a torpedo or bomb found its mark there would be no need for lifeboats.

Among those merchant ships was the SS *Induna* of 5,800 tons carrying a cargo of gasolene. On the morning of 21 March, the convoy slipped its moorings and steamed slowly out of the Iceland fiord to form into the ordered convoy pattern. They were on their way individually and on their own as a group of ships. There could be no turning back, no matter what punishment lay ahead. Tradition had been so established that no British seaman, Merchant or Royal Navy, considered retreat. The casualties might be high and the ships forced to part but in time the survivors if alive would arrive at their destination. In the long nights of impenetrable darkness, red-eyed lookouts and weary helmsmen peered into the inky darkness. No lights, not even a small torch could be shown, for somewhere out there in the night waters, German U-boats waited and watched for the passing convoy. The responsibility of steering even a moderate-sized ship, blind, in the middle of a fleet, grew from initial strain into mental torment.

The first light of a grey dawn found all the convoy still there but dishevelled and untidy, shuffling themselves back into station. By the end of the second day, things were going well, almost too well, until the elements took a hand. Away to the north, the sky had a peculiar livid colour; a dull purple tone, vaguely menacing, ominous. The sea had been building up inexorably all morning. Now at midday, dark and light grey-green waves, frothed with white tops, marched along like lines of soldiers.

The smaller vessels were already dipping their bows every ten seconds in a cloud of white foam, but, worse still, the temperature was falling fast. Up there, beyond the Arctic circle, the north wind blowing off the ice-cap can insidiously chill a man into a state of static numbness, into paralytic immobility. The sea rose very quickly, developing into enormous waves, marble-flecked with a translucent white-ness, rearing up into awesome mountains of water, rushing down on the ships as though to engulf them. As the storm increased, it seemed impossible that any man-made structure could survive the impact of so great a mass of relentless water.

By comparison, deep in the troughs, the quiet seemed unbelievable. Then followed the long haul, climbing slowly up to another foam-lashed crest, there to re-encounter the unbridled force of the tempest, tearing at everything and screaming like a thousand devils. At times, a giant among the rollers would break and come roaring down over the fo'c's'les, wrenching off anything not bolted down or not an integral part of the structure.

Heavy boats, well above the decks and held in place by grips, were snatched away like toys. Guard-rails became twisted and bent into grotesque shapes, storage racks which had once supported rows of rafts were rifled and emptied. Large reels that housed heavy steel wire hawsers used for towing other ships, weighing over a ton and fastened securely to the deck, were picked up like cotton-reels and catapulted through the air into the boiling sea. This was the Arctic at its worst. Conditions below decks were chaotic. Anything that was not tied or screwed down found its way on to the deck flooring to join the mass of gash (left-overs from meals) which shifted with every movement of the ship. In the galley, dinner-plates, cups, saucers and cutlery all tumbled and crashed to join the simmering pots of stew which had jumped off the hot stoves to mingle with the jumbled rubbish on the deck. By the third day, the gale had eased but not before it had achieved what the German Navy could not accomplish, complete dispersal of the convoy.

The nineteen merchant ships were now scattered over 150 miles of turbulent seas. The greatest chance of survival for any convoy under attack lies in its close formation and protecting screen of escorts. But now every ship was a straggler, on its own, totally unprotected and an easy target for a lurking U-boat. The destroyers were about sixty miles astern of the leading ship, rounding up what vessels they could find. Slowly but surely, the freighters discovered one another. Over the hours following the storm, the convoy developed into two separate flocks, one of nine ships and the other of five, seventy miles apart.

Five stragglers found difficulty in joining any group. The *River Afton* found herself near Narvik on the enemy coast, but succeeded in eventually reaching the Kola Inlet near Murmansk. *Empire Ranger* and *Raceland*, steaming ahead, were dive-bombed and sunk. Later on, the *Bateau* was also found and sunk by enemy destroyers. Meanwhile, in the far scattered group to the east, the large freighter *Induna* found herself alone in the vast area of the Barents Sea. Later on that morning of 26 March, she fell in with two other ships of the convoy, *Empire Starlight*, *Ballot* and the very small escort vessel the *Silja*.

About 3 p.m., the lookouts reported a lone plane approaching from the east. The poor visibility amid the incessant snowstorms made it impossible to establish its identity. It came in low on a steady course directly towards them. Among the officers and crews of the four ships, speculation grew with every passing second. Could it be a Russian plane sent out to look for a part of the missing convoy? Junker 88 bombers normally attacked from overhead, in a screaming dive, but this plane droned steadily on, holding its course on the starboard beam.

On the *Induna*, Gunner Jackson, with his crew of six at the Bofors gun, tightened his fingers round the trigger, his eyes lining up the target through the cartwheel sights. It would be foolish to take any chances. As the aircraft closed, it turned away to complete a tight circle around the four ships with the guns tracking it around. Jackson loved this gun, it was the best anti-aircraft weapon on the ship. Given half a chance, the slim 16-inch-long, three-pound shells could certainly destroy an aircraft. Jackson's suspicions grew with every passing second.

His number two gunner, also lining up on the target, kept repeating, 'On target ... on ... on ... on'. The plane turned again to make another approach at only 200 feet, levelling off at about 300 yards distant. As it did so, the visibility suddenly cleared. From somewhere on his right a look-out yelled, 'It's a bloody Jerry, he's coming in on ...'. The rest of the sentence was lost as the Bofors exploded into action.

The bombs flighting out from the bomb bay were momentarily parallel with the plane before lazily curling down towards the ship. They hit the water less than a hundred feet short of the starboard side of the hull, exploding on contact with the sea. But as the plane pulled up its nose, barely clearing the ship's masts, Jackson's gun spat out a concentration of deadly shells. The one clip of four shells was enough. The first round hit the engine cowling and ricocheted with a piercing whine; the second struck the starboard engine with a bright orange flash, followed by tongues of flame and thick black smoke, with the other two shells ripping open the fuselage. It was enough. Lurching sideways and rapidly losing height, the plane swerved violently away into a snow squall to disappear from view. There was no confirmation that they had brought it down, but the odds were much against it ever reaching its base in Norway. The instant elation which everyone felt after this success, was gradually dispelled and replaced by the sobering thought that the German pilot would without doubt have reported their position to German Command in Norway.

Early that evening, with weather conditions temporarily improved, three specks were seen on the horizon, and this sent the gun crews hurrying to action stations. As the ships neared, it was seen they were part of the scattered convoy, and as they took up station, they identified themselves as the *Effingham*, the *Dunboy* and the *Manna*. The little convoy was now made up of six merchant ships and the escort *Silja*. All through the next day, the 27th, they sailed on, hoping to meet up with others of the convoy. At 1.30 p.m. on the 28th, the sound of several aircraft could be heard overhead, but owing to the low cloud, nothing could be seen.

Then suddenly, a twin-engined plane dived out of the clouds and attacked the *Ballot*. The aircraft, a Messerschmitt 110, roared down in a determined attack with engines full on. At a height of about 500 feet, it dropped a stick of bombs before pulling out of its dive. Although not actually hitting the ship, the bombs literally slid down the sides of the hull. Exploding on contact with the water, huge waterspouts twenty or thirty feet wide at their bases burst in ear-shattering roars, pinnacling high above the masts. Minutes later another aircraft attacked the *Manna*, but in the meantime the *Ballot* was in trouble. The near misses had buckled some of her plates. Rivets had burst and seams opened flooding some compartments. The escort *Silja* circled for some time but as the convoy moved on, the two vessels became lost to view in a snow squall. By this time, the master of the *Ballot* had decided to play it safe both ways. He ordered sixteen of his crew to take to the lifeboats, while he organized the remainder into a damage control party to contain the flooding. *Silja*, still in close company, was soon able to pick up the crew in the lifeboat, and, with the assurance of the *Ballot*'s master that he could cope, turned eastward to rejoin the *Induna*.

During that evening, the captain of the *Empire Starlight* suggested to the captain of the *Induna*, who was also the Vice-Commodore, that they should steer further north and this was agreed. At midnight, Second Officer Mr Rowlands, taking over the duty watch on the bridge of *Induna* reported to the captain that they had come to the ice. The thin carpet of pancake ice made no appreciable difference to the speed of the vessels, which ploughed steadily on through the night. At least, it was thought, the danger from U-boats should surely be reduced in these waters. During the mate's watch between 4 a.m. and 8 a.m. events developed rapidly. The *Silja* came alongside and asked if they would give her a tow as she had now run short of fuel. It was also requested that *Induna* should take on board the men they had picked up from the *Ballot*'s lifeboat. This done, the *Induna* set off again steering due south.

As the hours passed, it became clear they had ventured too deeply inside the ice barrier. The thin pancake ice floes now gave way to really thick ice, which eventually became a solid field, and this brought them to a halt. With some skilful manoeuvring, the crew slowly worked the *Induna* around in the ice, broke free and then went to get the *Silja* clear. After going alongside, they took off the sixteen men of the *Ballot* and started towing again. By 3 p.m. the two ships were clear of the ice and headed for the Russian coast 250 miles distant. But with a rising sea and a freshening wind the weather worsened, and although *Silja* lengthened her tow line, the strain generated by these conditions parted the chain cable at 8 p.m.

After hauling in what was left of the cable, the *Induna* turned back to search for the *Silja*. Lights were flashed, whistles blown and the crew shouted, but they could find no trace of her. Because of the increasing snow squalls, there was nothing more they could do but proceed on their way. Although free of the ice-field, they were still close enough to it to assume that U-boats would hardly operate so far north. At their present speed another twenty-four hours would see them within reachable distance of the Russian coast. Although the lookouts were told to be doubly observant, no one noticed the telltale silvery wake of the periscope moving in on their starboard beam.

The U-boat commander must have viewed the scene with some degree of incredulity. A careful survey round the horizon showed him there was no other ship in sight – it was all too simple. No one even saw the track of the torpedo running shallow, its evil bubbling path lengthening as it rose to the surface to lie milkily along the dark green sea, before slamming into the starboard side well aft in no.5 hold with a tremendous explosion. This ignited the cargo of gasoline, and the resultant detonation threw everyone off their feet. Flames shot up to a tremendous height, and in seconds all the afterpart of the ship became a blazing inferno. With it came the noise of ripping tearing metal and the fatal sound of the sea flooding in under great pressure.

The two Bofors gunners who had just come on duty on the poop-deck, ran, jumping through the flames, until they were clear. The rest of the gun crews were still in their bunks on the deck below, and must have perished instantly.

Minutes after the alarm had sounded, the starboard life-boat was lowered. By the time Second Officer John Rowlands had destroyed the confidential papers and reached the boat, it was full – indeed it was overfull, for it now had to include the extra sixteen men from the *Ballot*. Each of *Induna*'s two lifeboats had a capacity of twenty-five men but now would have to embark thirty-three. From the deck, the chief officer ordered the boat to row away from the ship and lie off at about 200 yards. The other boat, although it had been lowered safely, was proving difficult to keep alongside. Those already in were being choked by smoke from the fire, fanned by a strong wind and blowing straight towards them. They were ordered to go around to the stern and take off the remainder.

As they were pulling away, the black dripping hull of a U-boat slowly surfaced about 100 yards away. It was a large craft, about 250 feet long, with a jumping wire and armed with a 20-mm gun forward of the conning tower. The men in the boats watched her, justifiably apprehensive, as stories had reached them of U-boat crews machine-gunning survivors in boats. In contrast, there were also reports of German commanders distributing provisions and blankets before bidding survivors 'good luck' when they left them. What sort of crew had fate given them on this occasion?

The submarine edged in towards the burning ship, firing a second torpedo which exploded in no.4 hold with a tremendous blast, lifting the ship and discharging a mass of debris into the air. As the boat crews waited, the stern of their vessel settled rapidly and the bows began to rise high out of the water. They watched in horror at the efforts of the remaining officers and crew to launch the small jolly boat, an impossible task as the falls had frozen.

In the confusion of the roar of escaping steam, internal explosions and the sound of inrushing water, the bows rose higher until they were almost vertical. Then, stern first, she plunged straight down, taking the men left on deck with her. From the time the first torpedo had struck, to her final disappearance, had been just thirty minutes. For some time, the U-boat stood off, then moving forward, submerged and was lost from view.

In the crowded starboard lifeboat, the men looked across the heaving sea for their comrades in the other boat. All they could see was an endless waste of tumbling sea. There was little time to hang about, for it was as much as second officer Rowlands could do to prevent the boat from falling into the troughs, broadside on to the waves, even when the crew were rowing as hard as possible. It was as well that the wind was astern and blowing them in the direction of their destination, Russia.

A sober assessment of the situation gave Rowlands little ground for optimism. They were about 175 miles from land, fully exposed to sub-zero temperatures in an open boat and subject to gales and snowstorms without warning. They were grossly overloaded and not only would the men be unable to take exercise to keep warm but attempts to row would be hampered. The boat itself was leaking badly and this, added to seas breaking over the sides, required constant baling to check the rising water-level. In his own mind, he had to admit it would be a race against time. How long could their bodies hold out against exposure to the wet and freezing air before they were rescued? Ice was already forming in parts of the boat. To the men, he presented a cheerful and optimistic picture of their chances; they had food and water, and the following wind if assisted by sailing and rowing would help them gain land. Those seated on the thwarts were the most fortunate, because the exercise of rowing kept the blood circulating. It was sheer hell for the rest. The injured lay on the bottom boards in freezing water. One of these was the donkeyman, who had been severely burned and was in great pain; every jolt of the pitching boat added to his misery. While most sat propped up against the sides, or perched precariously in the bows, the remainder managed to bunch themselves together in the stern.

Taking charge, Rowlands decided to hoist sail. Considerable time elapsed before they were able to step the mast and set the sail; the trouble being that he was the only one who knew how to handle a boat, as most were from the boiler-room. In this manner, the little band of survivors set out on their long haul to Russia. Although the boat was running before the wind, the men rowed in spells to keep as warm as possible. But when night fell, it grew extremely cold, with the temperature many degrees below freezing, causing hands to become too numb to grasp the oars. In the boat's lockers were seven bottles of whisky and these were passed around to combat the cold, with a warning to drink only sparingly. Unfortunately, some of the men drank a great deal of the spirit, and, becoming drowsy, fell asleep, several into too deep a sleep.

As the grey streaks of dawn appeared, those who had survived the night roused themselves to face another day. It was soon discovered that not only had the donkeyman slipped mercifully out of this life, but six of the older seamen who had drunk deeply the night before, were lying stiff and frozen and would not wake again. With the chill awareness that any one of them could suffer the same fate in the hours ahead, the remaining men lifted the bodies of their shipmates over the side and watched them float away. No one dared express the gnawing fear within their own hearts. All that day they sailed on, occasionally assisting their progress with ever-weakening attempts to hold and pull the oars. The insidious effects of frostbite were undermining their endeavours. None was wearing sea-boots, which meant that their feet and ankles were in water all the time. The foresail was unlashed and rigged as a shield against the wind and water on the weather side of the boat, which was fully stored with milk tablets, biscuits, chocolate and the like. Although they were not very hungry, the chocolate was appreciated and a few biscuits eaten. However, everyone craved water to drink. But the water in the containers, was, as might be expected, frozen into solid blocks, and the only way to get at it was to break open the canister and suck the broken lumps. Even the pemmican was frozen into unmanageable masses. This, like the water, had to be hacked into pieces with knives, not an easy task with frozen hands.

That evening, with the sharp lesson of the previous night very much in their minds, only a small sip of whisky was taken before settling down for the night. In the ensuing misery and discomfort of the swirling snow and biting wind, everyone felt the cold penetrating deeper and deeper. Early the following morning, 1 April, Rowlands' roll-call revealed that two more had died during the night. It was only with the greatest difficulty that the bodies were lifted and placed in the water.

> This little boat adrift in Arctic seas,
> These frozen men in which the germ of life scarce breathes,
> What courage when each hope has almost gone,
> To force the whispered cry 'we must hold on'.

As the day developed, they looked out over the turbulent water with growing despair, wondering just how much longer their bodies could withstand such exposure. From the original number, they were now down to twenty-three. While the second officer steered, the rest huddled together as best they could. In this way they could get some shelter from the wind and some mutual warmth from each other. A few men's legs had become so numb they were unable to move without assistance. During the afternoon, one of the greasers slumped over his oar and then rolled over into the bottom of the boat. An hour later, one of the four men in the bows, slid forward into a coma from which he never recovered. These two had to be left where they had fallen, as by now no one had the strength to lift them over the side.

As dawn of the fourth day broke, any hopes of seeing a coastline were dashed by the sight of the unbroken monotony of a heaving grey sea. Four more had lost the fight for survival during the night, leaving only seventeen alive. As the hours of daylight passed, and early evening approached with the prospect of another cold remorseless night, the last few shreds of hope were turning into an awesome fear. Only the hardiest men with the staunchest spirits could have lasted this long. Just before six o'clock that evening, one of the men in the stern pointed south, mumbling through cracked and swollen lips, something about a ship. All eyes scanned the dim horizon in the failing light and saw a tiny speck there.

Rowlands, using his binoculars with trembling hands, studied the object with all the concentration he could muster, the others watching him with quickening pulses. It was impossible to identify at first, for it was at least five miles away and was certainly not a ship. Then suddenly he realized what it was. Hardly trusting himself to speak, he turned to the others and said, 'Lads, we've made it, it's a lighthouse.'

In fact it was Cape Sviatoi lighthouse on the eastern coast of the Kola Inlet leading to Murmansk. Even in their extreme weakness they managed to reach out and clasp one another's hands. Too exhausted to cheer, the men wept openly. The adrenalin of hope ran through their veins like fire. Within minutes they heard the sound of approaching planes, low over the water. Soon, three Russian fighters were clearly visible, and, flying around the boat several times, they acknowledged the flag which the crew held open, before returning to the coast to bring help. At eight o'clock, just two hours later, a Russian minesweeper came alongside to take them aboard, but their numbed and swollen legs gave them no power to stand. The earlier exhilaration had drained the little strength remaining, to leave them frozen effigies of living beings. In this helpless state they could not get themselves out of the boat and the Russians had to come on board the lifeboat to fasten ropes and hoist them on to the ship. One by one, they were carried into a warm messroom, stripped and then wrapped in thick woollen coats and given hot coffee. The minesweeper, after setting course for Murmansk made a small detour during the night, and, while the rescued survivors of the *Induna* slept, the Russians came across another boat with survivors.

This turned out to be the port lifeboat. There were only nine remaining alive in this boat: the two gunners, five Americans, a fireman and a steward's boy. Shortly after reaching Murmansk, however, on 3 April, one of the Americans and the boy died in hospital. From the *Induna*'s total crew of 66 therefore, only 24 survived. After some weeks of treatment, six of these were able to walk and were later sent home to England. Many of the remainder, who were kept in hospital at Murmansk, had limbs so damaged by frostbite they became gangrenous. The overcrowded Russian hospital did the best it could, but some had to have arms and legs amputated. The operations were unbelievably primitive, for with no anaesthetic available, only some sort of deadening solution could be slopped over the limb before surgery began. The Russians were not to blame. Scanty medical supplies were rapidly being used up by the demand of their own massive casualties. Although the last ship of the convoy arrived in the Kola Inlet on 1 April, it was not until two days later that the arrival of the last survivors allowed this tragic chapter to be brought to a close.

3   The Sinking of the
ss *Empire Howard*

In the spring of 1942, with the number of merchant ships in
each convoy increasing, it became necessary to augment the
number of armed escorts. By this time, Hitler was becoming
progressively alarmed at the amount of war material being
convoyed through the Arctic, reaching the Russian ports of
Murmansk and Archangel for onward transit to Moscow.
His armies were suffering several setbacks on the Russian
front, in part, simply because Soviet troops were fighting
back with the vast amount of war material being supplied by
the United States and Britain.

As a result, many more bomber planes were sent to
Nazi-occupied Norway to supplement the strong Luftwaffe
already established at Banak and Bardufoss airfields, near
North Cape. The U-boat fleet was also increased and heavy
capital warships moved into fiords close to the Allied convoy
route, ready to move out and to strike at a moment's notice.

On 8 April 1942, a convoy of twenty-three merchant
vessels set out from Iceland bound for Murmansk loaded
with war materials for the Soviet Union. Of these, ten were
British, nine American, three Russian and one Greek,
accompanied by a small escort of anti-submarine trawlers
and a few minesweepers, intending to rendezvous with a
strong escort of destroyers and the cruiser HMS *Edinburgh*.
But from this point onwards the convoy ran into trouble. The
icefield around Iceland was further south than usual, and

several of the freighters and their escorts, lumbering through thick fog, crashed into floating block ice, causing severe damage to bows and hulls.

Six of the escorts were so badly mauled, they had to return to Iceland. Such was the confusion that a tense situation developed. In the hours that followed, the heavily laden merchant ships found themselves surrounded by, and colliding with, large slabs of solid ice, and with the situation worsening, there was a danger of being engulfed. It would have been hazardous enough in good visibility but here in this blanket fog, it became a nightmare. Now they were in the ice-field, they had to get out, but which way? Ruptured plates to the hulls caused flooding, bows caved in and the propeller blades were ripped off. A bad beginning to a convoy voyage on which so much depended.

By the time the weather cleared, only eight freighters were present, the rest having returned to Iceland. But these eight now had a most impressive fleet of armed escorts, comprising six destroyers, four corvettes, four minesweepers and two armed rescue trawlers, in addition to the cruiser HMS *Edinburgh*. With seventeen warships protecting the eight freighters, expectations of a trouble-free voyage ran high. Four days later, the convoy found itself just south of Bear Island close to the ice-barrier and it was here that the U-boats launched their attack. The destroyers played their part magnificently, and it was only by the constant dropping of depth charges that the enemy was forced on to the defensive and made to keep his head down. Because of the growing danger around them, Commander Maxwell Richmond, commanding the destroyer *Bulldog* ordered the merchant ships to make a spirited alteration of course to the south. It was a wise move, for it eliminated the danger of becoming involved in the ice-field, and allowed them to dodge the U-boats and mines laid by the enemy in the predictable path of the convoy.

Acknowledging the signal, the Commodore of the merchant fleet, Captain Edward Rees, DSC, RD, RNR, aboard the cargo vessel *Empire Howard* loaded with 2,000 tons of military equipment, immediately passed the order to the rest of the convoy fleet. *Empire Howard* had a displacement of 7,000 tons and had been built at Port Glasgow. This modern steamship had the traditional bridge amidships, two masts and a single funnel.

As the line of signals fluttered out from the Commodore's ship, followed by the 'Execute' flag, the vessels slowly turned into line heading south, the propellers violently churning the sea into white trails, toiling under the weight of their heavy cargoes. In the meantime, the destroyers were dashing around with bow waves creaming back, slicing through the dark grey sea, dropping pattern after pattern of depth charges on and around the lurking U-boats. Meanwhile, the convoy plodded on at the pre-determined speed of eight knots, a necessary pace in order to conserve fuel for the 2,000-mile voyage across the Arctic and through the Barents Sea. At this time, the freighters were in a formation of four columns each of two ships, with *Empire Howard* in the forward column. The wind from the north-east was blowing strong and steady, with the barometer falling and the snow flurries increasing. It was at this point that several U-boats daringly revealed their presence by surfacing some distance away. It has never been established whether this was a deliberate ploy to lure the destroyers away, but when Captain Rees saw the escorts racing off in pursuit, he remarked to Captain Downie of the *Empire Howard*, 'I hope the escorts are not being decoyed away from us'.

At that moment, the only close escorts remaining with the freighters were the two little armed anti-submarine trawlers, *Northern Wave* and *Lord Middleton*. But, unseen, one of the U-boats closed in on the merchant fleet and, after selecting as its victim *Empire Howard*, fired three torpedoes. Clearly visible, their long milky trails lay along the surface while the deadly missiles sped on homing in on the ship. The first plunged into the starboard side with a blinding flash and, five seconds later, the second burst through into the engine-room, while a third smashed into the magazine exploding in a massive eruption of flame and smoke. With the centre of the vessel torn out, the ship split in two. Such was the force of the explosions that the upper decks entirely disappeared and with them the heavy cargo of army trucks. As they fell into the sea, there was a rending roar of fragmenting machinery.

The crews of the nearby ships rushed to the rails staring in horror and disbelief. There was no hope for the ship, and *Empire Howard* began slipping into the sea stern first. Within seconds the taffrails were dipping. Twenty, thirty men were seen slipping, sliding down the tilting decks. There was no time to reach the lifeboats even if any survived. Within the next thirty seconds, the water was level with the bridge ladder. Captain Downie snatched up the confidential books stored in lead-weighted bags and threw them overboard. Then, wearing a life-jacket, he calmly stepped into the freezing sea and swam away a few yards before turning to watch the dying moments of his ship. In that brief span of her death throes, there was the roar of tons of water racing through the ship, tearing away bulkheads, smashing open watertight doors buckled by the blasts, pulling her pitilessly down and down by the stern into the waiting Arctic.

Second by second the tilt increased until she was almost vertical with her bows pointing to the grey sky as though in supplication. And then, with almost irreverent haste, she slid under to disappear among the expanding pool of black fuel oil and wreckage, from which gouts of air fountained and spurted. Slowly the turbulence subsided until finally, amid the flotsam that had vomited to the surface, no more bubbles appeared. Only sixty seconds had elapsed from the time the first torpedo struck. As the smoke cleared, Captain Downie saw that a number of the crew were clinging to bits and pieces of wreckage. In the heavy swell, a survivor swept past him. It was the Commodore, Captain Rees, casually trying to smoke a cigar, a resigned smile on his face. As the two men tried to reach one another, a large wave parted them, carrying Captain Rees out of sight, never to be seen again. Thus died a brave man, who faced the inevitability of death with a dignity and fortitude given to few.

At this time the sea temperature was at freezing point and

in these conditions the men should have been dead in seven minutes. However, the hundreds of tons of thick black fuel oil in which they struggled undoubtedly kept them alive. At the time the torpedoes hit the ship, the two little rescue trawlers were half a mile astern. They immediately sped towards the sinking vessel, their purpose twofold: to attack the lurking U-boat and to rescue survivors. The *Northern Wave* was the first to arrive. Immediately ahead, thrashing about in the sea, among the debris and oil, were thirty-eight survivors frantically waving their arms, shouting, pleading to be saved. The young captain was suddenly faced with a grave and frightening decision.

The delicate ASDIC-dome beneath the hull of his trawler had been damaged and put out of action in the icefield at the start of the voyage. He therefore had no means of establishing his conviction that the U-boat was in the depths beneath his ship, still circling around waiting to torpedo another vessel. To attack with depth charges in the area where the men were swimming and where the U-boat was probably lurking, would almost certainly kill many of them. Should he fail to attack, the U-boat would escape and more ships be sunk. Within his mind, he reasoned that the killer submarine had to be in the depths below the ship, for so little time had passed to allow it to make a clear getaway.

No man could have been faced with a more agonizing decision, which, as the seconds passed, cut into his heart and mind like a devil's scalpel. His orders on taking command of *Northern Wave* had been precise, clear-cut, 'Attack and destroy, the convoy must be saved'. Did this mean that to destroy the U-boat, he must if necessary sacrifice British lives? What in God's name was he to do? Their Lordships at Admiralty, sitting in their comfortable leather chairs, would undoubtedly have propounded with a profusion of well-meaning platitudes that this was all part of the war at sea, that it was his command, and this was the sort of responsibility that went with the job. Now in this terrifying instant of time he was expected to play God, to make the decision between life and death.

The shock realization that the fate of these men, wildly flailing about in the water, rested on his shoulders made him feel urgently sick. Even all the wisdom of Solomon and the philosophy of Socrates together could surely have found no answer. If he made no attempt to destroy the enemy and another ship were to be torpedoed and more men killed, he would be charged with 'dereliction of duty'. Racked by the mental torture of the judgement he would have to make, he turned to the crew, standing by the already primed deadly missiles and gave the order 'Fire depth charges'. For the rest of his life he would remember their faces. Almost to a man they registered astonishment and disbelief that they were being ordered to perform what was in effect the execution of their fellow comrades of the sea.

As the firing rings were pulled, the missiles catapulted from the ejectors, ten in all, plunging into the sea, where each would explode at varying depths of 150 and 250 feet. Never would he forget the shock and sorrow in those grey masks of faces, men who cursed bitterly, silently, some weeping openly, glaring at him in utter condemnation. For men in the sea in close proximity to depth charge explosions, there is no chance whatsoever; the result is inhuman, abominable, loathsome. Such is the frightening power of the sudden underwater expansion from 450 pounds of Amatol that the body is dismembered in an instant.

Moments later, in a sequence of ear-splitting explosions, the sea erupted into great pillars of water, spurting high over the dark sea. Only those furthermost from the explosions survived. Mercifully, those nearest died instantly, ripped apart by the shock waves, the details hidden in the flurry and roar of the blast.

As *Northern Wave* approached closer, it could be seen that some, still in their life-jackets, floated on the surface, bobbing up and down in the Arctic swell, staring with unseeing eyes. Even for those still alive, time was running out, for as the trawler ran on to start the rescue operation, engines were stopped and the telegraph rung to 'full astern', but owing to some malfunction, the engines failed to restart. It seemed that ill-luck was still dogging the convoy.

Down below, frenzied efforts were being made to start the machinery and to get the shaft turning. The trawler, by this time, was in and drifting through the area of water where some were still alive. It was here, as they approached a raft with six survivors, that a line was thrown and held. But the trawler was still drifting onward and the raft, still secured, was dragged aft under the stern, close to the propeller. There was a moment of instant panic, for, if the engines suddenly started, the blades would have cut them to pieces. To avoid this, the order was given to cut the rope and to cast off. Unaware of the reason, those on the raft stared in disbelief, thinking they were being abandoned. As the trawler drifted further and further away, despair replaced hope, howls of anger the earlier elation. By this time, the second trawler *Lord Middleton* had arrived, hauling the living aboard barely conscious. Meanwhile, *Northern Wave* was still drifting on, with another ten minutes passing before the engines were restarted, and, because by this time she was some distance away, another fifteen minutes elapsed before she returned to recommence her rescue attempts.

For those survivors who had drifted some distance, a sea boat was launched for a final search but when no more could be found, the two trawlers set out to rejoin the distant convoy. Aboard *Northern Wave* and *Lord Middleton*, everything possible was being done to revive the eighteen rescued men. Barely conscious, they were in extremely poor condition. With wet clothing removed, they were wrapped in blankets and carried into the warm engine-room, and, in a lifesaving bid to restore circulation, given brandy and whisky.

Only five minutes later, the two trawler captains received a signal from the surgeon-commander of one of the Royal Navy escorts – 'On no account are spirits to be given to the survivors'. But it was too late. Some had already fallen asleep, but it was a sleep from which there would be no awakening. Medical experience has proved that cardiac failure is the result of administering spirits. The medical report states that:

Although the giving of spirits would appear to have been the most reasonable remedy, the loss of body heat from such exposure slowly produces a state of hypothermia. In this condition, the periphery blood vessels shut in an attempt to maintain the core temperature of the body. Intake of alcohol opens the blood vessels, forces the skin vessels to dilate and the blood, rushing into the cold surface tissues, is further chilled and on its return, lowers the body core temperature still more. As a consequence, the temperature of the heart muscle drops, the fibres fail to contract normally and this in turn leads to cardiac failure.

Dr Philip Slater
Falmouth Surgery

From *Empire Howard's*'s original crew of fifty-four, only eighteen were hauled out of the sea alive, and of these nine died from the effect of the spirits given. Although *Northern Wave*'s captain stayed to search the area in the hope of finding some evidence of the U-boat's destruction, there was nothing, nothing except the sound of slurping fuel oil and floating wreckage, and bobbing corpses in life-jackets, moving rhythmically to the motion of the waves. Some time later, with her nine dead aboard, a heavy-hearted, embittered crew, a deeply distressed captain, the ASDIC-dome defunct, and no further hope of destroying the enemy, the ill-starred trawler joined the eastward-bound convoy for Murmansk. Once again, it was the Merchant Navy who had paid the price of merciless war.

4   The CAM Ship –
Empire Lawrence

Within German Naval High Command in May 1942, there was an atmosphere of jubilation at the news that Britain's latest and most modern cruiser HMS *Trinidad* had been sunk in the Barents Sea, following closely upon the sinking of the 10,000-ton cruiser HMS *Edinburgh*, with millions of pounds worth of gold bullion aboard her (which she had collected at the Kola Inlet). They were prepared to admit the loss of their two heavy destroyers Z.26 and the *Hermann Schoemann*, but weighed against the British losses, the scales came down heavily on the side of the Germans. It also strengthened the argument Grand Admiral Raeder had always maintained, that air-strength in north Norway was the best method of preventing convoys getting through to north Russia. His frequent appeals to Hitler to direct the Commander-in-Chief of the German Air Force, Reichsmarschall Hermann Goering, to increase the number of aircraft under Air-Command Norway, had eventually proved successful. Considerable reinforcements of bomber aircraft were sent, including the giant Condor reconnaissance planes, for they were able to fly long sweeps out into the Arctic Ocean to find the convoys and guide the bomber squadrons in to mount their attacks. As a result of these forays by the enemy, considerable losses were inflicted on the convoys with many merchant ships and their crews being destroyed. The First Sea Lord, Admiral Sir Dudley Pound, agreed with the judgement of the Admiralty that convoys should be halted until winter darkness set in to give some cover.

However, in the political arena, a different opinion was emerging. In October 1941, Lord Beaverbrook and Mr Averell Harriman had signed an agreement with the Russians in Moscow that specified quantities of war material would be delivered through the Arctic by June 1942.

Despite British losses, the Russians demanded that the agreement should be honoured. The Americans had in fact made available all the goods and the ships to carry them to meet the promised date. In Iceland and the United Kingdom, there were now 106 merchant ships, fully loaded, waiting to be escorted to north Russian ports, a fact which President Roosevelt was careful to point out. For Mr Churchill, it was a time for momentous decisions. In view of the British losses, he had to explain to the President the impossibility of speeding up the number of convoys in order to reduce the accumulation of freight ships. Escorts could not be transferred from the Atlantic routes to leave Britain's supply line unprotected. He urged the President not to press him beyond his judgement in the matter, until a solution had been found. But only two days later, the pressure was increased by a request from Stalin that every possible effort should be made to ensure the safe arrival of the convoy merchant ships now waiting in Iceland, as supplies were urgently needed for the Russian front.

In reply, Mr Churchill pledged that the Royal and Merchant Navies would fight their way through the Barents Sea with the maximum amount of war material. But the price of honouring such agreement was to fall most heavily upon the merchant ships in the succeeding convoys. It was therefore as a result of this weighted political pressure and in an atmosphere of apprehension that the decision was reached to send the next convoy codenamed PQ16.

PQ16 left Iceland on 21 May, comprising thirty-five ships with a close escort of four rescue trawlers, five destroyers, five corvettes and four cruisers, while units of the battle-fleet cruised between Iceland and Norway ready to intercept the

(Above) The ice-covered deck of the 'Dido' class cruiser HMS *Scylla* in the Arctic 1942. With parts of the deck machinery frozen solid, the use of steam jets is the only answer (Below) Gale conditions as seen from the bridge of HMS *Sheffield*. On one other known occasion, massive waves pushed the 500-ton 'A' turret of the cruiser *Trinidad* down through the forecastle deck rendering it useless

A near miss by a Stuka dive-bomber in the Arctic in May 1942

Part of a three-hour attack by sixty Stuka dive-bombers which succeeded in sinking the British cruiser *Trinidad* in the Arctic on 15 May 1942

The Blue Funnel line ss *Cyclops* which was torpedoed and sunk by
U-boat 123 near Halifax, Nova Scotia, on 11 Jan 1942 with the
loss of many lives

A destroyer launches a torpedo attack on the enemy. The 21-inch
diameter 'Whitehead' torpedo travelled at approximately 40 miles
per hour and carried a lethal warhead of 750 lbs of high explosive

Grand Admiral Karl Doenitz. He was successively Commander of German Navy's U-boat force, Commander-in-Chief of the German Navy and last head of the German government, May 1945

The U-boat 426 sinking during an attack by a Sunderland flying boat. From the start of Admiral Doenitz's U-boat campaign to its final defeat, a total of 780 German submarines were destroyed by combined Allied sea and air operations

Captain John Walker RN, flag officer commanding Atlantic convoy escort groups, the ace-killer of German U-boats who bears the distinction of having done more than any other to win the Battle of the Atlantic

The end of a torpedoed freighter in mid Atlantic. One of the many hundreds of Merchant ships sunk by Admiral Doenitz's U-boat campaign in World War Two

The famous oil tanker ss *San Demetrio* sailing up the Clyde after being shelled by the German battleship *Scheer*. Consumed by fire, her heroic crew of only sixteen men, brought her back across the Atlantic, complete with her cargo of oil, a distance of 1,500 miles

Parts of the Stuka dive-bomber on the deck of the tanker ss *Ohio*. This was one of two planes which crashed on to the ship

Captain D. W. Mason.
Captain of the tanker
ss *Ohio*

The petrol-laden freighter ss *Waimarama* blowing up after being hit
by bombs from a German aircraft

Concentrated bombing on the Malta convoy by German and
Italian aircraft

Anxious eyes watch the sinking carrier HMS *Eagle* after being
torpedoed by U-boat 73. The ss *Glenorchy* in the foreground was
torpedoed and sank two days later

(Top) MV *Rochester Castle* and MV *Dorset*. Of these two, only the badly damaged *Rochester Castle* survived to reach Malta *(Centre)* The SS *Ohio*, SS *Melbourne Star* and SS *Waimarama*. Only the *Ohio* and *Melbourne Star* survived *(Below)* The freighter SS *Clan Ferguson* carrying 2,000 tons of aviation spirit and 1,500 tons of high explosives. Shortly after this photograph was taken, a Heinkel torpedo-bomber scored a direct hit on the vessel

The Italian destroyer *Colleoni* hit by shells from HMS *York*

The exploding of the *Colleoni*

The aftermath of the *Colleoni* explosion

Winston Churchill with South African Prime Minister General
Smuts viewing the fleet at Alexandria

The blindfolded captain of the Italian submarine *Cobalto*,
Lieutenant Raffaele Amicarelli, being handed over to the army at
Gibraltar. The *Cobalto* which attacked the Malta convoy was sunk
by the British destroyer *Ithuriel*, commanded by Lieutenant
Commander Maitland Makgill-Chrichton, DSC

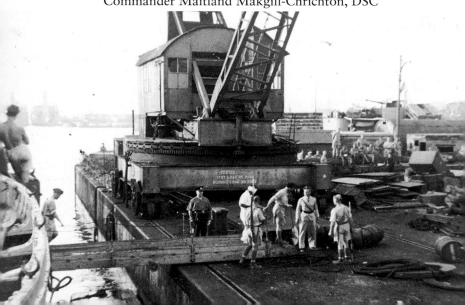

German battleship *Tirpitz*, should she move out to intercept the convoy.

The weakness of the plan however, was the absence of fighter protection. By early morning of 25 May, the convoy had reached a point to the south of Jan Mayen Island, and here Rear-Admiral Burrough with his cruisers and destroyers joined the convoy to give them support until the limit of his patrol was reached near Bear Island.

In this convoy was the merchant ship *Empire Lawrence*, a CAM vessel, the initials standing for Catapult Aircraft Merchant. It was in effect, an ordinary cargo ship, aboard which a catapult had been fitted and from which a Hurricane fighter plane could be launched. Its main purpose was to destroy German shadowing aircraft which normally circled the horizon reporting the convoy's course, speed and position, thus enabling U-boats and aircraft to intercept. But once the Hurricane pilot had performed his task, he had to come down into the sea, praying he would be rescued before freezing to death. It was a one-shot fighter plane.

At mid-evening on that day, the first of the aircraft attacks developed. Flying low over the sea came twenty-five Heinkel torpedo planes, while above them, peeling off from 15,000 feet with their spine-chilling shrill whines, dived fifteen Stuka bombers. For the next thirty minutes, the air was filled with the fearsome crump of bombs in and around the convoy and the intense barrage of gunfire from the combined firepower of escort and merchant ships.

In the middle of this battle, the Hurricane pilot on the *Empire Lawrence* decided that conditions and visibility were ideal for him to take off, and do something to reduce the effectiveness of the attack. Roaring away from the catapult deck, he climbed high into a suitable position on the port side of the convoy to begin his assault on the enemy. During this gallant undertaking, he dived in and out of enemy formations, firing his guns until the barrels grew hot as a constant stream of shells blasted into the fuselages of Heinkels and Junker aircraft. Ahead of him, a torpedo bomber, unaware of his approach until a hail of bullets killed the pilot, swerved violently, its wing tip hitting the sea and somersaulting in a flurry of water and flame to disintegrate into small pieces. Banking steeply away from the flying debris, and climbing rapidly he turned to his right, to see, below him, a formation of five Junker aircraft preparing for an attacking run on the convoy.

Roaring down from 10,000 feet with two enemy planes pursuing him, he tore into the group with fingers pressed tightly on the firing button. From the leading plane there was a sudden flash, and with smoke pouring from its engine, it turned away flying low over the water. In a panic of confusion, the remainder broke off in an effort to escape. But by now, with all his ammunition used up, it was time to return and to try to save himself. Signalling to the convoy that he would fly down the centre of the fleet and bale out, he approached from ahead and prepared to ditch. Unfortunately, two American ships astern of *Empire Lawrence*, mistaking him for an enemy plane opened fire, severely wounding him in the legs. Subjected to attack by foe and friend alike, he must have wondered what sort of war he had got himself into. Accelerating out of the hail of gunfire from the convoy, he again circled round, and coming in on the port side of the ships, baled out. As he floated down to drop into the icy sea, his plane crashed some distance ahead to disappear below the surface. It was speedy action by the destroyer *Volunteer* that succeeded in rescuing him before he succumbed to the sub-zero temperature.

In the meantime, while this isolated air battle was going on, the remainder of the enemy planes had regrouped and again began their attacks. The intensive barrage of gunfire put up by the escorts and by the DEMS (defensively equipped merchant ships) gunners on the merchant ships was such that the enemy was forced to keep away at a respectable distance. But a few planes did try to penetrate the defence screen, one even flying down the middle of the convoy at about 1,000 feet despite being repeatedly hit. Having reached the forward line of ships, it banked steeply and crashed about a mile ahead of the leading vessel. By now, the convoy had moved into an area of even more serious trouble, into a concentration of U-boats intercepting its course. Despite the speed and alertness of the destroyer escort, a few submarines managed to slip through the screen and approach the merchant ships undetected. There, they torpedoed the freighter SS *Syros*, which slowly sank allowing twenty-eight of her thirty-seven crew to be rescued.

During the afternoon the radar detected a large concentration of aircraft approaching from about fifty-five miles distant, and at 7 p.m. the assault commenced, with about sixty planes taking part, comprising torpedo, dive- and high-level bombers, pressing home their attack with determination. The first ship to be sunk was the SS *Alamar*, followed quickly by the USS *Mormacsul*. Minutes later, the Russian tanker *Stari Bolshevik* received a direct hit in the bows and was set on fire. The crew, which included women, fought the flames with great courage, refusing to abandon her. As a result, the ship, with a column of black smoke pouring from her decks, managed to rejoin the convoy.

But there were other disasters. Near misses by heavy bombs badly damaged the American *City of Joliet* and the British *Empire Baffin*. One of the most tragic misfortunes occurred when the Polish destroyer *Garland* received a saturated bombing attack as four bombs fell directly towards her. The first fell close beside the ship, which exploded and detonated the three others in the air. All the gun crews were hit by a mass of steel splinters leaving the decks covered with dead and wounded. Some hours later, another attack developed in which the ammunition ship *Empire Purcell* was hit by two bombs and began to sink. Only seconds after the crew had taken to the boats, the ship blew up with an ear-splitting roar and a mushroom of flame and smoke. Seconds later, a torpedo plunged into the hull of the *Lowther Castle* which quickly sank.

At one o'clock on the following day, radar detected another large formation of aircraft approaching, and thirty minutes later the attack began. Two groups, each of three planes, singled out the *Empire Lawrence*, and dived to 1,000 feet before releasing their bombs. The first two whistled over the bridge and exploded in one of the forward hatches blowing a huge hole in the ship's hull. There were two lifeboats, one on each side, and both of these were lowered to be clear of the water, as there was too much way on the ship to lower them directly into the sea. But while this was happening, the second group of planes dropped their bombs from just above mast height. Four exploded in the engine-room and into the after-deck, creating an enormous explosion as the magazines blew up. No merchant ship built could have received so much damage and still floated. Blasted by the impact, the *Empire Lawrence* split in two and began to sink rapidly by the head.

The explosion destroyed both lifeboats, killing and terribly wounding all aboard. The few that remained alive, clinging to bits and pieces of wreckage waved and shouted for help from the passing freighters but for a ship to stop in convoy would spell disaster. But worse was to come, for as the survivors of *Empire Lawrence* splashed around in the icy sea, three Stukas swept in low, just above sea-level, like messengers of death, pouring a stream of bullets into the helpless groups. These Nazi pilots of the so-called glorious Third Reich, indoctrinated by Adolf Hitler's ideology that 'terrorism and mercilessness are absolutely essential', were carrying out his programme to the letter, and seemingly enjoying it. Having performed their deed of execution, the sea rapidly became stained with the blood of their victims. As they sped away at full throttle with the screaming roar of their powerful engines growing fainter and the thunderous crash of the convoy's defending guns lapsing into silence, the only sound to be heard were the moans and cries of the wounded still holding on. Minutes later, the rescue trawler *Lady Madeline* and the corvette *Hyderabad* were on the scene to begin the task of hauling aboard the few who remained alive. Few indeed, for the casualties had been tragically high. But even while this rescue was in progress, the Commodore's ship, the SS *Ocean Voice* was torpedoed and set aflame but managed to maintain her position in the convoy; and, by some courageous efforts from the crew, the fire was brought under control. During the next three days, there were sporadic attacks by enemy bombers which failed to score any hits. With every hour that passed, anxiety grew about the lowering of ammunition stocks, and a signal was passed throughout the convoy to apply the utmost economy in its use.

On the afternoon of Saturday 30 May the convoy reached the outer entrance to Murmansk where another heavy air attack developed, but Russian fighters successfully broke up the German assault. At six o'clock that evening the merchant crews were landed and marshalled together on the quay. Battered, tired, exhausted and shivering from the bitter cold wind, they huddled together, hoping they would soon receive the warmth, hot food and sleep they so badly needed. It was not until eleven o'clock that night that someone came along and escorted them to the local hospital where they stayed for three hours before being escorted back to the quay. At ten o'clock the following morning an official from the Ministry of War Transport came along and admitted that he did not know what to do with them. Eventually, they were transferred to an old camp and there for the next six days lived on ersatz tea made from pine needles and fat pork, before being returned in small parties in homegoing convoys.

That the major part of convoy PQ16 survived the gruelling ordeal, despite the loss of, and the damage to, so many ships, and brought their vessels into the Russian port, was in no small measure due to the gallantry and heroism of the crews of the merchant vessels and the efficiency of the escorts. The gunners on the merchant ships behaved magnificently throughout, with the crews keeping them supplied with ammunition without any fear or panic, under the most heavy bombing and torpedo attacks. It was this spirit which continued to manifest itself during the remainder of the convoy voyages to Russia until the end of hostilities.

5 The Commodore's Ship – The SS *River Afton*

The convoy conference took place as planned at Hvalfiord, Iceland, on 27 June 1942. No palatial chamber this, just a large wartime hut barely accommodating the fifty or so men who had crowded in to receive sailing orders. On both sides of the long table, masters of merchant vessels and captains and commanders of Royal Naval escort ships sat listening to plans and strategy formulated by Admiralty in London. The merchant skippers had left their cargo vessels anchored offshore groaning under the weight of tanks, guns and planes, destined for Archangel to aid the Russian armies.

Here in Hvalfiord, they were meeting one another to discuss convoy problems. The older, experienced skippers listened politely, while the inexperienced, hastily promoted to fill casualty lists, made copious notes, grave faced. One or two, uninterested, individualistic, yawned their way through the meeting, or resolutely read a newspaper. They were among the early sinkings. The man who shouldered the greatest responsibility sat near the centre, listening to every detail. Commodore J.C.K. Dowding, DSO, RD, RNR, had no distinguishing features; he was a man who might pass unnoticed in a crowd. It was his eyes that begged attention, brilliant, keen, missing not one iota of detail. This convoy codenamed PQ17 was to be one of the largest to sail from Iceland, thirty-five freighters in all, loaded with 156, 492 tons of war material.

Dowding was to sail in the freighter SS *River Afton* and would be under direct orders from the destroyer escort, but in the event of an emergency the eventual safety of the convoy would become his responsibility. He, like the others, knew only too well the dangers that lay ahead. The 2,000-mile route passed north of Bear Island, due east towards the land mass of Novaya Zemlya, then south to Archangel. Once past Bear Island, the convoy would be in the most vulnerable position for attack from enemy aircraft, submarines and surface forces. And in this vast Arctic Ocean, with twenty-four hours of daylight at this time of the year, there would be no cover of darkness to protect them.

It was some consolation that the Admiralty would provide reasonable protection in the form of a close escort of six destroyers, four corvettes, three minesweepers, four anti-submarine trawlers, two anti-aircraft ships and two submarines under the command of Commander J.E. Broome, RN, of the destroyer *Keppel*. Mid-distant cover would be given by four cruisers and three destroyers, while long-range back-up would be provided by a force comprising the battleship *Duke of York*, the US battleship *Washington*, the carrier *Victorious*, two cruisers and fourteen destroyers.

Questions were asked about the mighty German battleship *Tirpitz*, anchored in a Norwegian fiord. It was true, confessed the chairman, that intelligent sources had reported that she and her escorts were moving very slowly north, taking full advantage of the cover provided by the many small islands along the Norwegian coast, but there was no evidence that she had, or indeed would, venture out to attack the convoy with the threat of heavy British forces waiting to engage her.

There were more questions and answers, more definitions and interpretations, and finally the meeting drew to its close, with the usual aphoristic platitudes of 'Good Luck'. Some handshakes, a few moments of conversation with old friends and it was over, each to his ship, each to his worries concerning the voyage that lay ahead. Commodore John Dowding had no illusions about the degree of importance attached to the enterprise and the cost in lives and vessels that

might have to be paid to sail this convoy through to north
Russia. His vast experience of wartime convoys had stemmed
from many Atlantic crossings in which he had somehow
miraculously survived numerous U-boat attacks. That had
been bad enough but the Russian convoys were infinitely
worse.

Back aboard the *River Afton*, Dowding, poring over his
charts, smiled wryly as he recalled the anxiety expressed at
the shore conference concerning the whereabouts of the
Tirpitz. The threat of this powerful ship provided ceaseless
misgivings to the Naval Chiefs of Staff trying to protect the
supply lines to North Russia. Snugly based in a fiord at
Trondheim, in Norway, almost invulnerable to attack, she
could at any time head out into the Arctic to intercept and
destroy a convoy. The presence of the *Tirpitz* at Trondheim
was also a constant source of anxiety to the Prime Minister,
Winston Churchill, who declared:

> The destruction or even the crippling of this ship is the
> greatest event at sea at the present time. No other target is
> comparable to it. Even if she were only crippled, it would be
> difficult to take her back to Germany ... the whole strategy of
> the war turns at this period on this ship, which is holding four
> times the number of British ships paralysed.
>
> *Churchill's Second World War, Vol VII*

While the Prime Minister and the Naval Chiefs of Staff
may have been concerned about the threat of the *Tirpitz*,
mused Dowding, it was nothing to the anxiety felt by convoy
captains and crews who would be on the receiving end of a
bombardment from the great battleship if she decided to
attack. The only thing preventing her from carrying out the
threat was the presence of the heavy British force constantly
at sea waiting for the chance of an engagement. On that same
evening, the convoy of thirty-five merchant ships, with a
total of over 2,000 crew, set sail for Archangel, leaving the
coast of Iceland a thin line against the horizon. Creeping
around this barbed coast during the first two days, however,
the ships ran into thick fog, bringing the first casualties. The

freighter *Richard Bland* broke formation, hit the rocks and was badly holed. Hours later the tanker *Grey Ranger* and the cargo vessel *Exford* were damaged by submerged ice, all having to return to port. By the 29th, the convoy had rendezvoused with Commander Broome's fleet of destroyers and corvettes and set course eastward.

A mighty armada this, fifty-five ships in nine columns covering an area of twenty-five square miles, each vessel in its planned numbered position; *River Afton* as Commodore's ship being the leading vessel in the ninth column. A stirring sight indeed, with signal flags fluttering from halyards, fussy little destroyers bustling around the perimeter of the convoy, or dashing up through the lanes, summoning ships into line, or encouraging a straggler to catch up. From his position on the bridge, Dowding watched with a mixture of admiration and apprehension. The convoy included ships of many nationalities and types.

There were big ships and little, old and new, dignified freighters, tankers with their volatile loads and rusty old tramps. All were essential, different in appearance but with a common purpose – to keep the prescribed speed and position. Most carried deck cargoes, piled high and chained down to withstand the inevitable heavy seas that would sweep across the decks. There was freight of every description, guns, bombs, planes, machinery, trucks, tanks, food, iron ore and medical supplies. They had no speed except that of the slowest, the most modern ship could only plod along like the oldest, a perfect target, a duck that must not fly.

Almost incongruously, the distant sound of cheering filtered across the waters. Through powerful binoculars, Dowding searched the rear of the convoy. It was as he thought. The smallest ship, an old tramp, was of necessity doing her party piece, a fluctuating performance. For the moment she had a full head of steam and had come charging up through the lines to the sound of ribald cheers as each ship was passed. Two miles further on, she predictably ran out of power. Once more the ships overhauled her, but this time the cheers were to urge her on. As he watched, one of the vessels seemed to be lost momentarily in a slight haze, and following the line he cursed at what he saw. From one of the ships in the fifth column, black smoke was erupting as from a factory chimney. An unforgivable sin in convoy, and a bonus for any reconnaissance plane miles away. At once, one of the destroyers came round in a tight circle at speed, racing up the line with a fountain of waves creaming back from the slim bows, heading for the offending vessel.

It slowed beside the freighter with orders shouted from a megaphone. Although too far away to hear what was being said, Dowding imagined there would be some pretty ripe language. Such carelessness was criminal, it put the whole convoy at risk. There was no need to advise the enemy of their arrival; he would find them soon enough. Almost predictably at noon on 1 July, the convoy was located by an enemy shadowing aircraft which kept its distance, circling around the horizon, reporting back to its base. As it was now only a matter of time before the enemy struck, the unanswerable question racing through the mind of every member of the crews was 'what were the chances of survival'.

It was in this atmosphere of tension that Dowding and the skipper of *River Afton*, Captain Charlton, having checked that everything possible had been done to meet whatever emergency might arise, gazed out over the steel grey waters of the Arctic and waited. Of the crew of fifty-six, there were seven Royal Naval gunners and two military gunners manning the ship's eight guns of varying calibre. Although the *River Afton* was an elderly lady, with none of the refinements of the modern freighters, she could produce a nice turn of speed if called upon, but this would be of little use now; convoy speed had to be governed by the speed of the slowest ship and not for them would there by the cover of darkness when the convoy might change course to elude its pursuers. Instead, the midnight sun hung poised along the rim of the horizon, and as one day merged into the next, it climbed slowly out of the Arctic sea.

It was not until 1800 hours the next day, 2 July, that the

first air attack took place. Five Heinkels, each carrying two torpedoes, approached the convoy on the port side. But here, they met the combined anti-aircraft fire of the escorts. This concerted firepower proved too much for them, and although they managed to drop their torpedoes, it was done in a desperate attempt to escape destruction. By dexterous manoeuvring, all the ships managed to avoid being hit. As the planes flew off, two were seen to have smoke pouring from the fuselages as they made for home, while another crashed into the sea about a mile ahead of the convoy. As the plane sank, a few of the German crew managed to scramble into an inflatable dinghy. With a sense of begrudging admiration, the crews of the leading ships watched as another Heinkel flew low over the water to land close to the dinghy, pick up the survivors and fly safely away, despite the target gunfire from one of the destroyers racing in.

On the following day, a major attack was developed by about thirty aircraft. They came in low from the south, circling in clockwise formation, organizing themselves for the fight. Having reached a position on the port beam, they turned and flew in to attack the stern of the convoy, intending to fly up through the columns of ships. Immediately, escort and merchant ships opened fire. The curtain of flak produced by this concentration of guns proved almost impenetrable. Plane after plane burst into flame, turned away or with smoke pouring from their fuselages, crashed into the sea. In the event, only four aircraft managed to complete the run through the convoy to drop their torpedoes independently. They flew between the third and fourth columns at mast height, raked by Oerlikon and Hotchkiss gunfire.

As the leader drew abeam of *River Afton*, a hail of flak from its guns blasted the plane, and swerving sharply, it hit the sea barely 200 yards ahead. From the enemy's point of view, the price of the assault had been high, for of the thirty aircraft taking part, twenty had been destroyed. But the attack had not been entirely unsuccessful. As the last of the planes disappeared over the horizon and the convoy regained its course, it was seen that three ships had been torpedoed and were sinking, the *Christopher Newport*, the *Navarino* and the *William Hooper*; and a fourth, the Russian tanker *Azerbaijan* had been badly damaged. Now it was the turn of the accompanying rescue trawlers to recover from the sea those who had survived the attack. Despite these losses, it seemed to Commodore Dowding and to Captain Broome in *Keppel*, that provided ammunition held out, they might survive any further attacks the Luftwaffe might make.

But while this attack on the convoy had been in progress, 2,500 miles away in London, a naval conference was being held, which was to determine the fate of the PQ17 merchant ships and their crews. In a room at Admiralty, the First Sea Lord, Admiral Sir Dudley Pound, and a number of senior officers responsible for convoy operations, sat discussing an emergency situation suddenly arisen, which, though foreseen as a possibility, provided no adequate solution. Before them lay a chart of the Arctic Ocean showing the position and course of our covering fleets and the convoy, and their estimated whereabouts at corresponding hours. Tension had developed with the receipt of intelligence reports that the German battleship *Tirpitz* with a supporting fleet had left its anchorage in Norway. It was proceeding north and might well be steering in the direction of the ill-fated convoy, which, they estimated, could be reached by midday on the following day. There were three possible decisions.

One, to order the convoy to return westward, and for the distant British battle fleet to steer towards it at speed until the two units were within air defence range of one another, which would be at about the same time as the German ships might arrive. This however, would have left the British fleet exposed to the whole might of the Luftwaffe in Norway, with only one aircraft carrier, whose planes would have been no match for the superior striking power of the enemy.

Two, to leave the convoy to continue its course with the close escort of destroyers in the hope that in the event of attack, the cover of fog or the use of a heavy smoke screen, some ships might avoid destruction. This second option, would have the advantage of keeping the ships together for concerted defence against further air and possible U-boat attacks.

And finally, there was the option of ordering the convoy to scatter in the hope that the German fleet would be unwilling to stay long enough in the area to round up odd ships over a vast track of sea, with the knowledge that British capital ships might cut off their retreat. Inevitably some would be sunk but a large proportion might escape.

The argument against this last plan, was that once the convoy scattered there would be no possibility of reassembling it, and therefore any unity of defence against air or U-boat attack would be lost.

It was clear, therefore, that threat of attack by the *Tirpitz* was the overriding factor in the First Sea Lord's deliberations, and, despite all arguments against, he reached the conclusion that the right solution would be to order the convoy to disperse. As a result, Rear-Admiral Hamilton, commanding the near cover fleet of cruisers and destroyers, and Captain Broome, with the close escort, received the signal, 'Immediate, owing to threat from surface ships, the convoy is to disperse and proceed to Russian ports', and this was followed by the second signal, 'Most immediate, convoy is to scatter'. From this it was assumed that an attack by the powerful German forces was imminent.

For Captain Broome, it was a heartrending decision to have to inform the Commodore and to leave the convoy to find its own way to Russia wholly unprotected, yet his instructions were clear. Because of this imminent attack by an enemy fleet, superior in force to the ships he commanded, he was to withdraw and in the absence of any specific orders, join Rear-Admiral Hamilton's cruiser squadron. The order to scatter his convoy left Dowding stunned. Under the impression that a major error had been made in signal communication, he twice asked for it to be repeated. When confirmed, he was led to the natural conclusion that an attack by the German ships might occur at any moment.

One can imagine the depths of despair into which masters

78

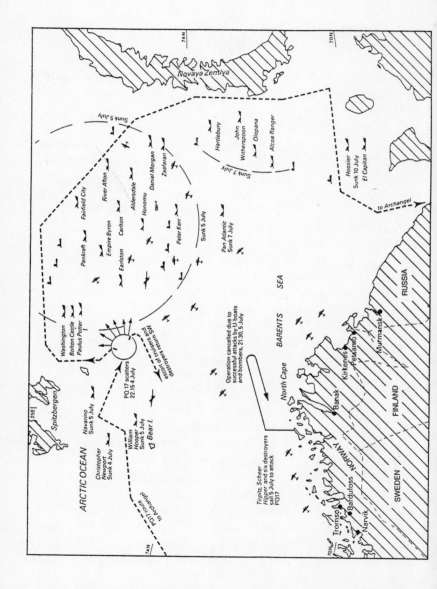

Fig. 2 The massacre of Convoy PQ 17, 4–10 July 1942

and crews of merchant ships were plunged as they watched the protective force of destroyers disappearing over the western horizon. It was a moment never to be forgotten in naval history. From the mast of *River Afton* there now fluttered the fateful signal 'Execute'. Immediately, each of the vessels turned and set an independent course.

Some vessels steered north towards the ice-barrier, others went south-east, while the rest fanned out at varying points of the compass in the general direction of their destination Archangel. From information received from their shadowing aircraft, it was not long before German High Command fully assessed the situation and decided to take full advantage. For them it was almost too good to be true. Here was one of the biggest convoys ever sent through the Arctic Ocean being abandoned by the escorts, left to fight their own way to north Russia. Never would there be a better opportunity than this to annihilate the entire merchant fleet.

Tirpitz, Scheer and *Hipper*, with an escort of eight destroyers, had indeed sailed north to intercept the convoy, after Admiral Raeder had finally obtained Hitler's permission to sail. The Chancellor, however, was not prepared to allow his precious ships to become involved in a head-on confrontation with the British fleet, and it was made perfectly clear to the Admiral that the foray was to be purely a hit-and-run affair. Within a short time of this meeting, however, news was received that the British close escorts had left the convoy and returned to the west, leaving the merchant fleet wholly unprotected. German High Command in Berlin now realized there was no point in risking German surface ships to carry out the destruction of the convoy when it could adequately be dealt with by aircraft and U-boats, and as a result, *Tirpitz* and her consorts were ordered to return to Norway. By now, German air force bases in Norway were humming with activity as squadrons of aircraft were taking off, heading north hunting for the naked convoy.

Under the leadership of Major Blodorn at Banak and Colonel Ernest Roth at Bardufoss, the strength of the Luftwaffe in the North Cape, Norway was now 411 aircraft of all types. Far out in the Barents Sea, every available U-boat began to converge on the merchant ships, hurrying, scurrying in all directions. The hunt was on, the extermination about to begin.

It started the following morning, 5 July. Among the early victims was *River Afton*. Both Commodore Dowding and Captain Charlton were in agreement that their best policy was to head north and keep as close to the ice barrier as possible, but here, they met packs of floating ice which were in danger of holing the ship. As a consequence, they were forced to steer eastward and were soon in trouble. While in position 76 degrees north and 43 degrees east and some 200 miles from the large island of Novaya Zemlya, they were hit on the port side by a torpedo from one of the marauding U-boats. Almost immediately the ship began to settle. From the bridge, Captain Charlton saw that the port motorboat was hanging in two pieces from the davits and large pieces of machinery were lying about the deck, blown out from the engine-room where the torpedo had struck. On the after-boat-deck, most of the crew, who had survived the explosion, were trying to lower the only remaining lifeboat from the starboard side. They had just succeeded in bringing it to the waterline with men in it, when a second torpedo hit the ship. The explosion shattered the boat, killing every man in it and all those on the boat-deck. The after end of the ship was by now a shambles for here, the 4-inch gun had been blown away and all the gunners killed.

The ship was settling slowly by the stern, and, having shouted the order to abandon ship, Captain Charlton collected his briefcase with confidential papers and made his way to the small dinghy, where he found several of his officers already alongside the ship with some of the crew. This little craft now had thirteen people in it and, being so overladen, the water was almost level with the gunwale. Unfortunately, the boat was being towed along by the way of the ship, with the forepart being dragged under, but as the painter was cut, the boat fouled the wreckage of the port motorboat throwing everyone into the icy water. The second and third officers managed to grasp the lifelines hanging from the boat deck and regain the ship.

The chief officer, who had his duffel coat on, was floating but unable to swim due to the water collecting in the sleeves and hood of his coat. Captain Charlton heard him calling for help but, owing to the weight of the case on his back and the extreme cold, it was all he could do to keep himself afloat and to struggle to the upturned boat. One of the seamen, A.B. Hanford, attempted to reach the chief officer, but he too got into difficulties and had to abandon the attempt. Several members of the crew had managed to get away on four rafts, and some of the men from the dinghy were able to swim and reach the rafts.

In the meantime, Chief Steward Grey, who had remained behind after the ship was abandoned to tend to the injured members of the crew who had no hope of reaching the rafts, also made his way down into the flooded engine-room with Chief Engineer Edward Miller. They pulled to safety Second Engineer Wood, and having put him on a stretcher, pushed him away from the ship and towards one of the rafts.

With him was Second Cook, Albert Waller, who, after assisting the Second Engineer to the raft went round the ship distributing life-jackets to some of the crew. At this moment, a third torpedo struck the ship. The explosion brought a terrific flash created by the torpedo hitting explosives stored in that area. For some minutes clouds of smoke and debris blotted the ship from view, but as it cleared it was seen that the vessel had broken in two, and seconds later, she disappeared. It was now assumed that Grey had perished but to everyone's astonishment he was seen to be swimming his way among the floating debris and eventually reached one of the rafts. Waller was never seen again.

Second Engineer Wood had already been on three previous convoys and had volunteered for the fourth trip. This time he was trapped in the engine-room when the first two torpedoes struck. Although badly injured in legs and spine, with the aid of the rescue party he was hauled up and put on to a raft, but, as the third torpedo struck, he was blown into the sea. There, he managed to cling on to a floating hatch cover, and was later pulled back to the raft where he died from his injuries and exposure. He was a gallant officer whose bravery and cheerful example were outstanding. Minutes later, another submarine broke surface near them and the periscope of one was sighted some distance away. The submarine closed on one of the rafts, and Able Seaman Marsh was taken on board and asked the ship's name. Having revealed it was the *River Afton*, he was given a bottle of water and some bread, and, after taking a photograph of the survivors on the raft, the German captain told them the course and distance to Novaya Zemlya, and ordered the submarine away.

Those who had survived grouped their rafts together and discovered that of the fifty-six aboard, twenty-two were missing. Among those surviving was John Dowding, sitting on a raft with three of his staff. Numb with cold from their immersion in the icy water, exposure began to take its toll and soon some could neither speak nor move, but a few hours later, when hope of rescue had been abandoned, the smoke of a ship was seen on the horizon, and, with flagging spirits momentarily revived, flares were burned and seen by the approaching vessel.

As she neared, she was recognized as the British corvette HMS *Lotus*. The survivors were picked up and given warm clothing and food; they arrived at Matochkin in Novaya Zemlya the following evening. The sinking of the *River Afton* was but one example of the saga of the destruction of convoy PQ17, where courage, sacrifice and endurance emerged as the common element.

Another early victim was the *Empire Byron*, torpedoed by a pursuing U-boat. About the same time, and a little to the north, four ships in company were attacked and sunk by the combined efforts of U-boats and dive-bombers. These were the *Earlston*, the *Washington*, the *Bolton Castle* and the *Paulus Potter*. Only minutes later the *Pancraft* sailing alone was sent to the bottom, followed by the *Carlton*. Later that day, two more freighters, *Fairfield City* and *Daniel Morgan*, were attacked and sunk. Four others suffered the same fate –

the tanker *Aldersdale*, the rescue ship *Zaafaran* and two freighters, *Peter Kerr* and *Honomu*. For a while there was a lull in the massacre, but the following day the attacks recommenced. The *Pan Atlantic* was set on fire and sunk, and the U-boats in the eastern sector of the Barents Sea, aware that remnants of the convoy would be heading for Novaya Zemlya as their last hope of survival, raced ahead to intercept, and waited. One by one, the pathetic little freighters appeared over the horizon and sailed on into the sights of the waiting periscopes. *Hartlebury* went first, followed by the US, SS *Olopana*, the British *John Witherspoon* and the *Alcoa Ranger*.

A few ships managed to reach the anchorage of Matochkin, which separates the two halves of the huge island of Novaya Zemlya. When Commodore Dowding arrived in HMS *Lotus*, he found five of his fleet there with two anti-aircraft ships, three minesweepers and three rescue trawlers. If discovered, they would have been a sitting target for air attack, and as a result they formed a small convoy and headed south for Archangel in the hope they would reach that port without detection. But two days later on the evening of 9 July, when less than sixty miles from the coast, they were attacked by forty dive bombers.

Despite appeals to the Russians to send out aircraft to protect them, no such help was forthcoming, and for the next four hours they were subjected to precision bombing, resulting in the sinking of two more ships, *Hoosier* and *El Capitan*, and serious damage to two others. In this attack, the enemy lost four bombers from the accurate fire of the accompanying anti-aircraft ships. Late on the following day the little band of merchant vessels and the few escorts arrived at Archangel, to find that two ships had already arrived, the *Donbass* and the *Bellingham*. Only five ships survived out of the thirty-five that had sailed from Iceland thirteen days earlier.

Gradually news filtered through that a few more ships had managed to reach Novaya Zemlya. Despite his gruelling experience two days earlier, Commodore Dowding began to organize a rescue force. His men must be found and brought back. On the 19th, a force of three corvettes, *Lotus, Poppy* and the French *Malouine* reached the southern half of Novaya Zemlya, where they found twelve survivors of the US, SS *Olapana* camped ashore. Eventually, reaching the Matochkin Strait, they discovered 5 more freighters with 200 survivors. Wasting no time, Dowding immediately got the convoy under way and after a final last lap, harassed by constant air and U-boat attacks, safely reached Archangel on the 24th. Among the survivors recovered at Novaya Zemlya were those from the SS *Hartlebury* of 5,000 tons, and from the report later submitted by her skipper Captain G.W. Stephenson, there emerges a remarkable story of courage and endurance against impossible odds. He states:

On the 6th July, when about 17 miles from Novaya Zemlya we were hit by a torpedo which struck the ship on the starboard side, under the bridge. There was a loud explosion and the ship shuddered violently. A large column of water was thrown up and we could smell cordite. As I rushed on to the bridge I was struck by falling debris. I was unconscious for a time and when I recovered found myself buried under pieces of decking from the gun platform. Just as I came round, I heard another explosion on the starboard side as another torpedo struck the ship in the engine room. The starboard boat, which was in the process of being lowered was blown away. About a minute later, there was a third explosion in the after end of the ship in No 5 hold.

This last explosion was the most violent of the three. I think the ammunition stowed in the after hold exploded, as I saw a large column of black smoke rising and could smell burning cordite. The ship immediately broke into three pieces. The main mast crashed and one man who was lowering the forward fall of the port lifeboat was blown away and the boat left hanging. By this time, both starboard boats had been destroyed. The lights had failed and all accommodation had collapsed. Fortunately, the three rafts were released and I threw a knife to one of the crew and told him to cut the after fall of the hanging port lifeboat which crashed into the sea and became waterlogged. I then gave the order to abandon ship, at which time there was only one man left on board with me, and we both jumped into the sea from the bridge deck, which was then only five feet above water. Only six minutes after the first torpedo hit the vessel, *Hartlebury* disappeared. Together, we swam to the waterlogged lifeboat to find one man already there, and having climbed in, found the water came to our waists. At that time, we were unable to reach the bailer or bucket to empty the water. We picked up several members of the crew and finally there were seventeen in the boat. Although it was foggy, I could see seven men on one raft and fourteen on another when the fog shut down visibility altogether. We did everything possible to get the boat cleared of water which was at freezing temperature but the conditions made the crew extremely cold and numb. Four men died during the first five hours, and we were unable to do anything for them. I took the lifejackets off the bodies and buried them.

Later we found a bucket, and with this, managed to get the water down to the level of the tanks. One by one, during the next twenty-four hours men died, and by that evening there were only four of us left; the rest having perished from exposure and shock. I have to report that after the ship sank, the submarine surfaced. It was large and had U.13 painted in black on the side of the conning tower, and round the 13 was a black horseshoe. The U-boat moved close to our waterlogged boat and I was asked if the Captain was a survivor. I told him no, and he then went over to the raft, and the men there, having thought I had been lost, told the German Commander so. He spoke to the Chief Officer and asked if he was a Bolshevik and on learning that he was not, he said – 'So what the hell are you going to Russia for?' The Chief Officer, having been told that many ships had been sunk from this convoy, was given the course and distance to Novaya Zemlya, a bottle of wine, another of gin and five loaves of black bread. The sub had a machine gun trained on us during this conversation, and was taking cine-photos of the men on the rafts as they were receiving the food etc. This commander had a red beard, spoke English fluently and was dressed in an ordinary peak cap and a coat similar to our duffel coats. After about five minutes, the submarine submerged and went off. Early on the morning of the 8th, I gave the crew some pemmican and biscuits and a small tot of brandy each. We rigged a sail and steered a course S.E. towards the land, which I estimated to be about sixteen miles distant. At ten o'clock that morning we picked up nine men from one of the rafts, and continuing ᴗur course at eleven o'clock that night, landed at a small inlet in Pomorski Bay at Novaya Zemlya.

The place was entirely uninhabited, so on landing, we rigged the sail as a tent, lit a fire and made some pemmican soup. We found a number of birds' eggs which we put into the soup and in spite of the eggs containing young birds, they tasted very good. Two days later, we sighted a vessel which appeared to be stopped. Launching our boat, we sailed towards her and found she was the American ship *Winston Salem* as she lay aground on a shoal. Boarding her, we found seven men from one of our own rafts on board, thus making a total of twenty survivors from our ship with the loss of thirty-nine men. A week later a Russian Survey ship arrived and transferred us to the MV *Empire Tide* and having been again transferred to the *La Malouine*, we finally reached Archangel on July 24th.

In the final count, out of the convoy of thirty-five freighters only eleven survived the terrible onslaught by the enemy's bombers and U-boats. When the extent of the catastrophe became known, reactions were highly charged and accusations of inexpediency on the part of the Royal Navy and mishandling of the situation by the Admiralty were levelled by people on both sides of the Atlantic. In retrospect, it was simple enough, at a later stage, to assess the overall situation and to know what should have been done but at the time, it was similar to two men fighting in the dark, each guessing the other's move. A decision had to be taken, and the responsibility for this rested on the shoulders of the First Sea Lord. There is little doubt that history will subject the judgement of Admiral Sir Dudley Pound to critical examination and logical disputation but less certain is that it will ever reach a satisfactory conclusion.

The weight of the many attacks on this convoy was reflected in the number of enemy units involved. Apart from the massive fleet of U-boats, over 200 bomber and torpedo-carrying aircraft fell upon the merchant vessels. It was a calculated and methodical system of slaughter, incomparable in maritime history. The stories of the men who survived are those of heroism and endurance amid a prolonged nightmare of suffering and torment over many days. In open boats, in freezing conditions and blizzards, some who were left alive from their sunken ships, had to row 350 miles to the nearest land of Novaya Zemlya. Many perished from cold and exposure.

The reports given by survivors help to illustrate to some extent, the appalling and shocking conditions which had to be endured in this and other convoys in the Arctic and Atlantic oceans, in their fight for survival after the fearsome experiences of enemy action. There are far too many to be included in this abridged account, but an example may be given, that of the bosun of the freighter *Empire Ranger*.

After being dive-bombed, the ship sank quickly and only one lifeboat managed to get away. Thirty-eight, including a fourteen-year-old cabin boy, were packed like sardines in this boat. For six days they were carried along by wind and tide, subjected to snowstorms, gales and the freezing wind. Each day took its toll. A Russian tug eventually found them drifting not far from the coast. Half-propped up in the bows sat an elderly seaman, his beard white with snow and frost, looking out across the tumbling sea, frozen into immobility, quite dead.

In the boat, huddled together, were the frozen bodies of thirty-six men. Only two were still alive. One was the cabin boy, David, a Scot from the city of Edinburgh. Stretched across him, providing warmth and protection from the snow and wind lay the bosun, more dead than alive. Although the boy's feet were in a dreadful state from frostbite, through long immersion in ice-cold water in the boat, he eventually recovered, but for the bosun, the bid to save the boy's life extracted a terrible penalty. The Russian hospital into which he was later admitted found that to save his life it was necessary to amputate both arms and legs.

The bosun was later able to reveal that on the fifth day of

their ill-fated voyage, when only four or five remained alive, fate had played an almost unbelievable last cruel trick. A swirling mist had descended on them fanned by a freezing breeze. As the fog grew thicker, it blanketed visibility altogether. Only the lapping of the water against the sides of the boat could be heard. Then suddenly, they heard a whistle. The sound faded, then came again, louder and more constant. Hearts raced with excitement. Surely it was someone from a rescue boat trying to find them. With little strength left, they tried to shout, but despite their efforts there was no answer. Still the whistle persisted. First it seemed to be astern and then ahead. The sound was eerie, almost supernatural. In their low state of mind, the mystery was deepening every minute, becoming almost frightening. Desperately their eyes tried to pierce the fog but found nothing. Moments later, their hopes were dashed when the riddle was solved. On the seat of the boat, gently rolling with the movement of the sea, lay an empty bottle. As the breeze swept through the boat, it played on the open end of the neck of the bottle, trilling the whistling sound. As the bosun said later, it was a time when hope turned to utter despair, the worst moment of their ordeal.

Following the fateful signal from the First Sea Lord, Admiral Sir Dudley Pound, that the Arctic convoy PQ17 must scatter, each of the thirty-five merchant ships set off at their best speed to various points of the compass, some sailing individually, others in little clusters.

Three freighters, *Silver Sword, Troubadour* and *Ironclad*, were in company with the little armed trawler *Ayrshire* under the command of young Lieutenant L.J.A. Gradwell, RNVR. They were then in an approximate position 76 degrees north, 29 degrees east. In the next few hours many distress calls from other ships of the scattered convoy could be heard over the radio as they were attacked and sunk by German dive-bombers and submarines. It appeared that most of the merchant ships were fleeing eastward trying to reach Novaya Zemlya, 500 miles distant.

By Gradwell's reckoning, a little over 100 miles to the north-west, lay the tiny island known as Hope Island, one of the loneliest, most dreary islands in the world. Why it was given the name 'Hope' remains a mystery. He considered that their best and only chance of survival lay in that direction. After discussions with the captains of the three freighters, the four ships set off, led by Gradwell's *Ayrshire*. Their intention was to anchor on the westward side of the island, out of sight, until the enemy threat, from which they had been ordered to retreat, had passed. But before reaching the island they ran into a sea of floating ice. As this became thicker, it was necessary to alter course.

Over the radio, they could still hear many distress calls from the doomed convoy ships as they fell victim to enemy attacks. Gradwell considered that, having reached thus far, survival lay in forcing a channel through the pack-ice. Followed by the freighters, and using his trawler as an ice-breaker, he penetrated some twenty miles before it became clear that further progress was impossible. Although this manoeuvre would prevent them from being hit by torpedoes, it made their ships not only immobile but also utterly vulnerable to air attack, for now the black hulls stood out against the dazzling white of the icefield, and once enemy aircraft spotted them their fate was sealed.

With the bows of the vessels pointing eastward, they were lying starboard side on to the south, the direction from which marauding enemy bombers could see them. There was only one solution – camouflage. It was, without doubt, Gradwell's logical thinking that saved them. Boarding each vessel in turn and rummaging through their stores, a number of tins of white paint were collected and the crews set to work painting the southern-facing hulls.

Bridges, hulls and superstructure of each vessel were thoroughly coated, making them almost invisible against the background of ice. All three freighters were carrying tanks as deck cargo and, as an added precaution, these were made ready for action, the necessary ammunition broken out and the breeches loaded. As a final safeguard, all fires were banked up, so that not even a wisp of smoke could escape to betray their position. For the next two days, the little cluster of ships remained silent, immobile, undiscovered, locked in the ice. When no more heart-rending distress calls were heard over the radio, Gradwell decided it was safe to move. But they now found they were ice-bound, for the driving wind had built up ice against the hulls of the ships. It was only by the power of the trawler and the strength of her steel bows, breaking through the ice, that *Silver Sword, Troubadour* and *Ironclad* were at last able to free themselves.

The question now arose whether they should set course for their original destination Archangel to the south-east or head north. In the event, Gradwell decided that as there might be greater danger steering towards Archangel, it would be safer to set course for Novaya Zemlya. Two days later, the four ships sailed into a natural harbour to the north of the island where they took stock of their situation. Further to the south, Novaya Zemlya is divided by the Matochkin Strait, and it was to here that *Ayrshire* led the freighters and found another of the scattered convoy, the *Benjamin Harrison*. A relayed message from the Russian signal-station in the strait in due course reached Commodore Dowding, which set him on his rescue mission from Archangel.

The conduct of the captain of *Ayrshire* was described by Admiral Tovey as 'a splendid example of imagination and initiative'. It was an opinion warmly endorsed by the masters of the three freighters which Lieutenant Gradwell had led so skilfully to safety.

6   The *Niger* Affair

By the spring and summer of 1942, due to the number of ships sunk by enemy action, many Royal and Merchant Navy survivors had accumulated at Murmansk and Archangel, awaiting passage home to Britain and America. In the first part of the Arctic war, all convoys sailing from Iceland to north Russia were given the prefix code letters PQ, and those returning QP, followed by the number of the convoy. By the end of June, these survivors were told that a selected number would be returning on the next westward bound convoy, codenamed QP13. Men of the sea are by nature superstitious, and those selected, on learning of the ominous convoy number 13, were clearly apprehensive.

There were certainly grounds for fear and pessimism. Only three months earlier, in April, the convoy PQ13, bound for Murmansk, lost not only five valuable merchant ships from enemy action but also the new 8,000-ton cruiser HMS *Trinidad*. In a battle with large German destroyers, she had by a million to one chance torpedoed herself. This was caused by the malfunction of the torpedo she had fired, which half-circled and returned to hit the cruiser amidships. She did however manage to keep afloat and to struggle into Murmansk for repairs. It was the only time in British naval history that a ship ever torpedoed herself in battle. Six weeks later, temporarily repaired, *Trinidad* set out from Murmansk on the night of 13 May, only to be dive-bombed in a mass attack, set on fire and sunk with heavy loss of life. In each of these events, the number thirteen had had sinister association.

The question the survivors at Murmansk asked themselves was, would this convoy QP13 also be added to the fateful list? The QP13 convoy which set out on 27 June comprised thirty-five merchant ships with an escort of five destroyers, four corvettes, two rescue trawlers and two minesweepers, one of which was HMS *Niger*. Of the 700 survivors from the cruiser which had been sunk on 2 May, about 400 were allocated places in the returning Royal Naval ships.

During the long period of their service aboard the cruiser and their enforced stay in the north Russian port, long-standing friendships had been established. When it was announced that the places allocated by Admiralty would be according to priority of requirement, it gave rise to much disquiet, for groups would be split up. Despite all the vociferous efforts for chums to be together, the Admiralty's policy was strictly adhered to. Unaware of the dramatic events that were to follow, selection or non-selection was to prove the difference between life and death. These rules also applied to merchant crew survivors returning in the thirty-five freighters, made up of sixteen British, seventeen American and two Russian, the latter having women and children aboard. The convoy had a quiet passage to Iceland in a calm sea, undisturbed by the enemy, the reason being in part due to a covering of fog but mainly because German Command was concentrating the weight of its attack on the ill-fated eastward bound convoy PQ17, of which twenty-four of the thirty-five ships were sunk. QP13 arrived off the north-eastern corner of Iceland on 4 July and, as planned, sixteen of the thirty-five vessels bound for Great Britain turned due south along Iceland's eastern coast.

The remaining nineteen, mainly American, set course for Reykjavik, making their way along the northern coast. Acting commodore for the American merchant ships, and leading the convoy, was Captain John Hiss, master of the freighter *Robin*. At this time of the year the Arctic has twenty-four hours of daylight and although thus far the weather had been reasonable it deteriorated into a stormy evening with a keen northerly wind. Scurrying clouds almost at sea-level, and drifting rain, reduced visibility considerably. These conditions prevented accurate navigational calculations, and the leading ships had only a vague idea of their position. But unknown to the American commodore and the masters of the merchant ships, a British minefield had been laid off the north coast of Iceland, extending across the Denmark Strait, in order to prevent German warships breaking out into the Atlantic to attack our shipping. Only a narrow channel barely ten miles wide lay between the southern edge of the minefield and Iceland's North Cape through which the ships had to pass.

In the poor visibility, HMS *Niger*, commanded by the senior officer of the escort, Commander Anthony Cubison, RN, sped ahead to establish a navigational fix, signalling the American commodore Captain Hiss to reform his convoy from five columns into two, to pass through the narrow passage. At this point it would appear that only Cubison and his officers were aware of the existence of the minefield. From soundings, Cubison estimated that Iceland's North Cape had been passed, and therefore ordered a westerly course to make a land sighting. Cautiously moving through the mist, he saw what appeared to be the shape of a steep cliff looming through the murk and assumed it must be part of the cliff face of North Cape.

If, indeed, this was correct, then the convoy had altered course too soon. Moreover, it presented immediate danger, for if this course was continued, the ships would soon be close to the rocks. To rectify this, Cubison urgently signalled Hiss to turn his nineteen freighters and steer due west. Such had been the reduced visibility that all this while merchant and escort ships had been streaming fog-buoys. This is an elementary practice in fog conditions, to prevent a following ship colliding with the stern of the ship ahead. A rope secured to a floating buoy is trailed behind the leading ship and this in turn throws up a fountain of water which can be seen by the following vessel. But on this new course, the whole convoy, unaware of the minefield, was heading straight for it.

Within minutes of the convoy swinging round on to the

newly directed course, a sudden clearance in the fog bank revealed to Cubison that what at first had appeared to be a cliff face, was in fact a towering iceberg. Realizing that they might be very close to or even in the minefield, he hastily signalled Hiss to change course and steer south. But it was too late. At exactly 22.40 that night, *Niger* herself hit a mine and blew up. The passengers and crew of the trawler *St Elstan* some 300 yards behind watched in horror as massive explosions rent the air, followed by a sheet of flame and smoke.

The vessels following and on either side, in one involuntary movement, veered away. *Niger* sank rapidly, the explosion having torn out her bottom. One moment she had been cautiously moving through the mist, the next she was nothing but a disintegrating wreck, disappearing beneath the waves, while deafened eardrums and stunned minds struggled to grasp the awesome horror of the event. As she tilted further and further into the sea, a muffled explosion shook the ship as her boilers burst and then, toppling over on to her side, maintaining a level with the sea, her masts and funnel dipped despairingly into a surface of burning oil spewed out from the tanks. For a few moments her shattered bottom gleamed black and stark against the sea, and then suddenly, amid great gouts of vomiting bubbles, she was gone.

With her she took Commander Cubison, eighty officers and crew and thirty-nine HMS *Edinburgh* survivors. For a while there was silence, a terrifying fearful silence, with the realization that this was no horrific nightmare; this was real. Amid and beneath the fast-growing pool of black evil-smelling oil lapped by flames, lay the comrades of those who watched. In an instant of time, their friends had become the victims of the very instruments of war intended for the enemy.

Meanwhile, still unaware of the real reason for the disaster they had just witnessed, the convoy steamed on, deeper into the minefield. Moments later, the freighter SS *Hybert* struck a mine and blew up with a great flash and, split in two from keel to superstructure, the two parts fell away into the sea, disappearing beneath the waves in a matter of seconds, leaving an ever-growing lake of burning oil. In the next few minutes, panic and confusion took over, as, in the on-coming convoy, one ship after another shuddered under the impact of detonating mines.

Each explosion triggered other mines, erupting huge fountains of water, which in the poor light, made them appear as splashes of shell-fire. In this nightmare scenario of shadowy light, driving rain, mist and the flame and smoke of exploding mines and burning oil, and still unaware of the minefield, captains and crews readily assumed they were either being shelled by an unseen distant warship or being attacked by a pack of U-boats. With explosions all around, they had no idea which way to turn. And then, two more freighters blew up, the SS *Heffron* and the SS *Marramar* both sinking in less than two minutes, leaving their crews fighting for survival in the pancaked ice water, clinging to pieces of floating wood.

The next to go was the SS *Randolph*. Running straight on to a mine, her bows were blown off, but with watertight doors closed and her bulkheads holding, she stayed afloat for some time resisting the rush of incoming sea. By now confusion was total. There was no time for the tidy emergency drills laid down in seamanship manuals, no time for signals. It was instead a bid for survival, every ship for itself, helms frantically pulled and wrenched to port or starboard, rudders responding with agonizing slowness, and the vessels themselves sluggishly turning and twisting in a frenzied bid to escape the unknown terror that lay somewhere out there, annihilating them one by one.

As another blinding flash lit the grey sky of the Arctic night, there came the roar of a massive explosion on the starboard flank. This was the Russian freighter *Rodina*. As she slewed round in a tight turn to port to avoid the ship ahead, a mine slapped hard against her hull amidships on the starboard side. The explosion blew away an extensive area of her plates, leaving a gaping hole through which the sea rushed. As it smashed through fractured bulkheads, it pulled her down and down into the cold dark sea. Within seconds, she listed heavily to starboard, still slewing round, the movement speeding her destruction by increasing the force of water. As she went over, her tilting decks were exposed to the passing ships. With her starboard rails dipping, she slid further and further into the sea, her decks packed with people savagely struggling to reach the lifeboats, among them many women and children. Although two boats drifted away empty, they were pitifully supporting up to thirty in the water, clinging with frozen hands locked over the gunwales. For those left on the ship there was little hope of survival. Those who could swim, jumped into the sea, not risking being dragged down by the inevitable suction. Others climbed on to the port side guard-rail, postponing for as long as possible the fate that awaited them.

As the vessel started to roll over, a few managed to reach the long keel, rising like a monster from the deep, gleaming wet black. It was only a momentary stay of execution, for, losing their grip, they slipped and slid down the upturned hull, their bodies torn and ripped by the barnacle-covered plates.

Amid a tumult of bubbling, spouting water, the ship was rocked by a massive explosion from somewhere deep within, drowning the screams and cries of those in the sea. Minutes later, amid the unforgettable sound of her death throes of gurgling, bubbling, steaming water, she slid lower and lower until only the keel lay along the surface. And then as the waves lapped across the bilges, she quickly disappeared from view, leaving a mass of human flotsam, thrashing about in the slurping oil, waving, crying, pleading to the passing freighters who had no intention of stopping, knowing full well that to do so would seal their own fate. But *Rodina* was not to be the last ship to be sunk that day for, immediately astern, the SS *Exterminator* struck a mine. This time, there was no fire, no smoke, no massive explosion, just a deep-throated internal roar that ripped open the bowels of the vessel. With her keel and midships hull torn asunder, her bow and stern rose sharply, V-shaped, centre dipping, hanging there suspended, vomiting her human cargo and black oil. As the two parts rose higher, she swiftly settled into the depths leaving a spreading area of struggling men.

At this time, the dead and the living in the sea were over four hundred, with *Niger* and six merchant vessels sunk out of nineteen. The two rescue trawlers *Lady Madeline* and the *St Elstan* dashing around in the middle of this carnage, also had no idea of the existence of a minefield, assuming like others, that either enemy warships were shelling the convoy or that U-boats were in the area at periscope depth picking off their victims. Meantime, the remaining freighters were lumbering around, not knowing which way to turn.

With the main body of escorts, destroyers and corvettes some distance away, the two trawlers were left with the responsibility of protecting the convoy. An almost identical situation now arose as with the freighter *Empire Howard*, torpedoed some three months earlier. Somewhere around and beneath them were lurking submarines, or so they thought. Unless they were destroyed, more ships would be sunk, more lives lost. A critical decision had to be made and quickly. If depth charges were fired, people in the sea would be killed, that was certain but if they stopped to pick up survivors the U-boats would escape.

But the captain of the *St Elstan* had already made up his mind. The trawler, sweeping around into the middle of the disaster area, fired a spread of charges. As the deadly missiles rocketed from the ship hurling far out over the water, a number were also dropped from the stern. At varying distances however, there were hundreds of people in the last stages of exhaustion, struggling to keep afloat, terror-stricken people, who seeing the oncoming trawler, waved and shouted and screamed, begging to be rescued. Even in the short time that had elapsed, scores of bodies from the sunken ships lay along the surface, or, fully lifebelted, bobbed up and down in the swell. Suddenly with ear-splitting blasts, the depth charges exploded, discharging columns of white foaming water high into the air. The effect on those swimming in the sea was shocking beyond description. The fortunate ones died instantly. The captain and crew of the *St Elstan* were convinced that even if the depth charges had not actually destroyed or damaged the U-boats, it would at least keep them submerged for a time, time perhaps to recover the living.

Moving around in ever widening circles, *St Elstan* began its search, still totally unaware of the deadly mines all around. To aid the process of recovery, scrambling nets were lowered over the side. Following the effect of the exploding depth charges and the exposure in such icy water, it seemed incredible that anyone could still be alive, but among those they managed to haul out of the sea were two of the HMS *Edinburgh* crew who had taken passage in *Niger*. Some in the oil had survived simply because of its viscosity and concentration providing a layer of protection, but for men in the sea, black fuel oil is an iniquitous, vicious thing. In a lopping sea, it is almost impossible not to swallow and the resulting intake burns the lungs, scorches the eyes and tears the stomach in violent bursts of retching.

One of the *Edinburgh* men taking passage in the *St Elstan* was Harry Cook (a colleague of the author). In an effort to save those in the sea, he and one of the trawler's gun crew went over the side in the scrambling nets, holding on by one hand, while at the same time trying to grasp and pull in with the other those still alive. Cook describes the event:

We brought in a total of sixteen altogether. The trawler was going around in circles trying to pick them up but many could not be reached. The waves kept sweeping them away out of our grasp. It was a very grim ordeal, as some of those in the water were women and children. These were the families of the Russian and Polish consul staff taking passage. I remember picking up a small child, finding it dead and letting it drop back into the sea. A few were able to climb up the netting themselves but all were soaked in oil, their eyes sealed and blinded and most were so utterly spent and on the verge of collapse, they could do nothing to help themselves.

During the rescue, a huge wave caught us both and tore us off the net, away from the ship, but the next wave carried us crashing back on to the ship's side and the netting, which we managed to grab. The skipper was furious. 'Get back aboard and that's an order.' We came across a boat with a few Russians in. They managed to climb on their own but left one man sitting alone in the boat, stark staring mad, shouting and screaming in his native language. We eventually managed to get him aboard and laid him on the deck, where he continued with his hysterical outburst. The Russians were so ashamed that one of their own countrymen should behave in this way, they went over and kicked him in the ribs while he was lying there.

Meanwhile, more escorts arrived and began picking up survivors. Among these escorts was the Free French corvette *Roselys* under the command of Lieutenant Bergeret. This corvette, with the trawlers *Lady Madeline* and the *St Elstan* manoeuvred around in the middle of the minefield for six and a half hours rescuing survivors, and in that time, picked up 230 out of the water, several of whom died later of exposure. Vice-Admiral Brayward, commanding the American Task Force, told Lieutenant Bergeret that he had earned 'the respect and gratitude of the United States Navy', for in that period of time, *Roselys* had steamed around in that dangerous area to save 170 men and women. Unfortunately, it can be seen from the following signal just how many died after being pulled from the sea.

Unless otherwise ordered, *Roselys* and *Lady Madeline* intend to proceed independently to Reykjavik at maximum speed, to land injured survivors from *Exterminator, Rodina, Hybert, Marramar, Heffron, Randolph* and *Niger.*
   Survivors are distributed as follows –
Roselys – 120 including 6 injured.
St Elstan – 23 no injured.
Lady Madeline – 40 including one injured.
                                   ETA *Roselys* 1630 GMT.
                                      The Review magazine
              (Naval Historical Collectors & Research Association)

While no figures were ever released of the number who perished in this tragedy, a conservative estimate must certainly be around 250.

7 The Battle of the Atlantic

In the Battle of the Atlantic during the period mid-1942 to mid-1943, the tide of war was flowing strongly in favour of the enemy. Admiral Doenitz's U-boat campaign was revelling in what German Naval Command described as the 'Happy time'. British merchant ship losses in the Atlantic from August 1942 to May 1943 rose to a staggering 1,974,000 tons, a total of over 300 vessels and the loss of many lives. It was upon the merchant fleet that the burden of cruel war was falling most heavily.

In practical and personal terms, the Battle of the Atlantic was a life-and-death struggle between the German U-boat and the British escort vessel. But it was also a bitter conflict between two men, each resolute in his purpose. Admiral Karl Doenitz, Commander-in-Chief of the German Navy, held the ruthless intention of destroying the Allied merchant fleet in the Atlantic and thereby cutting off Britain's life-blood of supplies to force her into surrender, and Captain John Walker, RN, Flag Officer commanding the Atlantic Convoy Escort Groups, held the equally firm resolution of defeating the German Admiral's purpose by all the means at his disposal: a trial of strength between two protagonists, each worthy of the other's steel, each firmly dedicated to his mission.

Doenitz was almost fifty years old when the war started, an old man by fleet standards. He had fought in World War I as a U-boat captain, and when his submarine was sunk in the Mediterranean in 1917 he was taken prisoner and sent to England. In 1935, he was appointed Senior Officer of the first U-boat flotilla and not only maintained that position to the end of the war but in the meantime, replaced Admiral Raeder as Commander-in-Chief of the Navy. There is certain symbolism in this man, for both world wars ended in his captivity. Fanatically dedicated to his career, he devoted all his efforts in the training and development of U-boats and their crews in the ten years he was responsible for them. From October 1935, he built up a highly efficient nucleus of trained personnel, and by 1937, his fleet was secretly performing attack exercises in the Baltic.

While all this was going on, the Admiralty in Great Britain was seemingly unaware of these developments and relatively unconcerned over the possible effect on our merchant fleet if, and when, the obvious impending storm of war did break. Even if they were aware of these exercises, they turned a blind eye. When war came in September 1939, Doenitz had few U-boats; by various means of coercion, demand and logical disputation, between then and the turning-point in the Battle of the Atlantic in May 1943, he had accumulated several hundred U-boats.

It is indeed a sobering thought that if Doenitz had been allowed to have control of U-boat construction and its production rate before World War II and to have had all the submarines he needed to fulfil his dream of a 300 U-boat fleet by 1939, he might well have starved the United Kingdom into surrender. This was Doenitz's 'Grand Strategy' and his single-minded purpose right from the start. There is no doubt that he was above all else, a specialist in submarine warfare. Apart from this asset, he equipped his headquarters at Kiel with the latest technical devices to gain priceless intelligence through the interception and decryption of Allied cypher messages.

From this he knew in advance the movement of Allied convoy shipping. Even right up to March 1943, unknown to the British, large amounts of invaluable information was reaching his headquarters, and he was therefore able to direct his U-boat packs to specific targets. It was an astonishing weakness indeed in British cypher security. In 1941, Great Britain had lost a total of 1,300 ships through enemy action of all types, but in 1942, U-boats alone sank another 1,300. These results created such enthusiasm and exuberance in the German camp, that Doenitz could smell the scent of victory in the air. So sure was he of success, and that Britain was on the point of collapse, he exhorted his crews to even greater efforts. He calculated that if these U-boat achievements in the Atlantic could result in sinking 800,000 tons of shipping per month, it would easily starve out the British. At that time in 1942, British shipping losses were running at around 650,000 tons, a figure far beyond the rate of replacement.

At the start of 1943, one of the most bitter battles of the Atlantic Ocean was fought in March of that year. Acting on intelligence gathered, after breaking into British convoy cyphers, Doenitz concentrated 39 U-boats against two eastbound convoys totalling seventy-seven ships. The U-boat attacks accounted for eight ships in eight hours, and altogether a total of twenty-one ships were destroyed with the loss of many lives. This convoy battle marked the high point in Doenitz's offensive, for it nearly achieved his dream of sinking ships faster than they could be built, and his long-cherished ambition to sever Britain's lifeline of supplies to force the country into surrender.

But from May 1943, a dramatic change took place in Allied fortunes, bringing to an end the U-boat 'Happy time', for during the next four months our shipping losses fell to 45,960 tons. In May alone, 40 U-boats were destroyed in the Atlantic. The reason for this extraordinary change of fortune can be explained by the Admiralty's transition to an entirely new form of offensive strategy against Doenitz's submarines. The success of this operation was in no small part attributable to one man, Captain John Walker, who was to become the ace-killer of the U-boat, a man Doenitz regarded as his personal enemy.

It was to this man and his unorthodox methods of war

against the enemy that many masters and crews of merchant ships sailing the oceans were to owe their lives. Walker's unconventional ideas to defeat the campaign of terror on the oceans were at first dismissed by the Admiralty, but his persistent application to be given a sea command and to be allowed to apply his theories in anti-submarine warfare was eventually granted. It was he argued, futile for escorts to collect around convoys and simply wait for the enemy to strike when he thought fit. He emphasized the need for setting up 'hunting groups', whose function it would be to adopt an offensive role at all times, seeking the enemy far away from the convoys. He put in a further plea for small aircraft carriers to accompany every convoy to fight off the ever-present reconnaissance planes. To all these proposals, the Admiralty gave the utmost consideration: much of which was approved. Success was immediate, and as his new revolutionary ideas were adopted by other escorts, the number of U-boat sinkings rapidly increased.

As time went on, it was clear that Doenitz was losing U-boats faster than the shipyards could build them. Furthermore, he was not only losing valuable trained crews but, due to the poor quality of partially trained personnel replacing them, U-boats were more easily falling victim to the new offensive methods applied by British escorts. The bitter Atlantic campaign which lasted over five years was fought with pitiless intensity, for upon its outcome depended the very existence of the United Kingdom and indeed the British Empire. These supplies sustained the defence of freedom, the ability to amass sufficient strength to carry the war to the enemy and provide food and other supplies for the home front.

Although Allied losses during the Nazi sea offensive were frightening, the price Germany paid for this temporary victory in all theatres of war was the loss of 1,060 of their U-boats, in which over 54,000 crew members were either killed or taken prisoner. By the end of hostilities, the life expectancy of a submarine and its crew was two missions.

In the worst period, 1942, anxiety in Whitehall over

Britain's shipping losses was demonstrated in the Central Operations Room, where a large graph recorded merchant ship sinkings in the Atlantic battlefield. At the top of the chart, a red line indicated the fragile margin between victory and defeat, for as long as recordings stayed below that line Britain's ability to survive and fight was possible. Once they moved above, showing vessels being sunk faster than they could be replaced, Britain's power to continue her fight in defence of freedom was in doubt. A sobering thought indeed when one considers that by the end of the war his U-boat fleet had sunk 14.5 million tons of shipping. In his memoirs, Doenitz appears not to have any conscience or to express any remorse over his savage attacks on Allied shipping and the massacre of thousands of Allied merchant seamen, but rather to regret that he had not destroyed many more ships with all the tragic consequences that would have entailed.

Ironically, Doenitz seems to impute the responsibility to Hitler, for despite his declared intention to bring Britain to her knees by his U-boat campaign, he skilfully sidesteps any responsibility for the atrocities committed by his U-boats and infers that he was influenced by Hitler's magnetic and powerful personality. He maintains that he himself was supremely conscious of this influence, and made every effort to get away and free himself from it. However, this attitude is contradicted by his constant visits to Hitler in the latter part of the war, in an effort to ingratiate himself with the German dictator whose announced dictum was 'terrorism is absolutely essential to victory'. It was this closer relationship with the Fuehrer which, following Hitler's suicide, led to him becoming Head of State, albeit temporarily.

It was during 1942–43 that the peak of the graph soared dangerously close to the red line, leaving the members of the War Cabinet with a numbing realization of the life-and-death battle being fought on the great Atlantic Ocean. It was a time when Chiefs of Staff were at their wit's end, trying to find an answer to the U-boat problem. But in May 1943 there came a dramatic change in Britain's fortunes. It was not attributable to any relaxation in the enemy's offensive but, as history shows, as a direct result of the navy's new strategy with the little escort ships and an air offensive.

July was a severe setback to Doenitz's ambitions for supremacy in the Atlantic, for during that month, in all operations over a wide area, no fewer than 37 U-boats were destroyed, showing the grand total since March as 121. One of the significant elements in these figures was his loss of over 6,000 trained crew members, some ending up in British prisoner-of-war camps. It was little wonder that among U-boat crews morale fell to an all time low, and that operational efficiency and endurance deteriorated. This was reflected in Britain's shipping losses, for whereas in March 538,000 tons were sunk, by July the figure had dropped to below 100,000 tons.

It was here that the very character of Doenitz asserted itself, for despite these setbacks he dug in his heels, refusing to accept any thought of defeat. In a desperate bid to regain the initiative, he launched an offensive by spreading nearly 150 U-boats across the Atlantic shipping lanes. However, this frantic endeavour was more than matched by Captain Walker's dogged determination to utterly eliminate the U-boat menace and to make the Atlantic safe for our merchant ships.

In order to understand the reason for Captain John Walker's successes and the thinking behind the methods he proposed and implemented which led to eventual victory in the Battle of the Atlantic, it is important to consider also his practical contribution towards defeating the U-boat menace. It is not intended to infer that John Walker alone won the Battle of the Atlantic, but rather to establish that it was his initiative, his original ideas, which, when adopted and carried through by all sections of the naval and air services, led to the collapse of the U-boat campaign.

Following the U-boat savagery of World War I, when Britain was almost defeated by the German submarine warfare, a secret body of scientists and experts in the field of anti-submarine activities set up an organization to combat such a menace in any future war. This was the

Anti-Submarine-Detection-Investigation-Committee, from which initials came the acronym ASDIC. Their research resulted in the discovery that a sonic beam directed underwater towards a submarine's hull could be bounced back and be measured to give a reasonable bearing and range. Exciting as the development proved, it had its limitations, for against surfaced submarines it was useless. Furthermore, when the attacking destroyer was immediately overhead, it failed to hold the submerged target, and subsequent depth-charge attacks had to be executed blind. Nevertheless, it proved to be an invention of outstanding significance.

By the mid 1930s, an anti-submarine school had been established at Portland, a branch of the Royal Navy then regarded as of little importance, unglamorous and unnecessary. No one at that time could have foreseen that it was this arm of the service that was to save Britain from disaster. Even Winston Churchill, in his *History of the Second World War*, accepts that he had often criticized the policy of, and expenditure on, the ASDIC research department, but admits that had not these experiments been vigorously prosecuted there would have been no answer but defeat. Commander John Walker, however, had an enduring faith in its future. A step in this direction came in 1937 when he was appointed as Commander of the Portland School, HMS *Osprey*.

During these pre-war years leading to the outbreak of hostilities, it became clear that war with Germany was inevitable. And while British statesmen like Stanley Baldwin and Ramsay MacDonald preached disarmament and Neville Chamberlain blandly proclaimed 'peace in our time', German rearmament grew apace and the war clouds gathered.

In his capacity as commander of the school, Walker, with his vision of the considerable influence that small escort vessels fitted with ASDIC would have to play, insisted that the U-boat threat in the coming war would become the key issue to Britain's defence. He constantly urged that his views be passed to Admiralty and that he be given command of his own ship. Almost twelve months passed before the Admiralty finally consented to his repeated applications, and in March 1941 he assumed command of the sloop HMS *Stork*, based at Liverpool. It was here that the Admiralty established its Western Approaches Headquarters to control the comings and goings of every convoy sailing in the Atlantic, the Mediterranean and the Arctic. Its main function was under the aegis of three departments; a Close Escort Group, an Intelligence Division intercepting U-boat signals at sea, pinpointing their positions, and a Coastal Command Group sending its aircraft over the convoy route to the limit of their fuel endurance.

It was now that Walker's experience and his faith in ASDIC was at last recognized by the Admiralty. To his delight, he was appointed Senior Officer to command the 36th Escort Group of nine ships, the sloops *Stork* and *Deptford* and seven corvettes, all fitted with ASDIC. Following weeks of relentless training, Walker built his team into an efficient fighting force and received approval from the Commander-in-Chief to adopt his plan for controlling the activities of U-boat attack at night. This entailed the firing of starshells and rockets (known as 'Operation Buttercup') to illuminate their presence, thereby forcing a surfaced U-boat to dive. Once submerged, their position could be confirmed by the searching ASDIC and the boat depth-charged. Great Britain's shipping losses from 1939 to the close of 1941 amounted to 430 ships being sunk with a gross tonnage of 2,162,170.

Walker became a legend in his own time, a man who by reason of his unorthodox methods of attack and despite limited support, achieved and laid the plans for ultimate defeat over Doenitz's U-boat campaign. In the first eighteen months of his sea command he had registered his sixth U-boat kill, an achievement unsurpassed in U-boat-hunting warfare.

For those U-boat Nazis captured by the Royal Navy in the war at sea, there was ever present an intense and fanatical hatred of the British. Many were a product of Hitler's Youth Movement, indoctrinated into a psychological loathing of their enemy before they even sailed. There were occasions in

World War II when British warships depth-charged their quarry to the surface and the survivors of the U-boat were hauled aboard as prisoners-of-war. Exhausted and wretched, they always appeared to be a rather insignificant lot, totally unlike the superhuman heroes hailed by the German Propaganda Minister Dr Goebbels; no glorified heroes these, just a party of inconsequential Germans. There was a report, unconfirmed, that on a certain occasion, one of several survivors from a sunken U-boat, having safely reached the deck of a British destroyer, pulled himself up to his full height and gave the Nazi salute with a 'Heil Hitler', only to have his foot heavily and accidentally trodden upon by Able Seaman Bloggs who happened to be passing at the time.

But for all these outstanding successes, Walker unknowingly was paying a heavy price. And the crews of the Escort Group were tiring. Endurance has its limitations, and there had been no moment when they could forget the danger that lay around them. From one dawn to another, there had been no sleep, little time for food and exhaustion lay heavily in the mess-decks and wardroom. Walker himself had taken the main burden. There, on the bridge of *Stork* he had sat propped up in his high chair on occasions for four days and nights without sleep. He was a tower of strength, holding everything and everybody together by sheer determination and personality. His presence on the bridge was essential. Officers and men alike needed the assurance of the man they trusted, a gaunt figure hunched in the tall chair, obeying the nagging voice that told him he could not, dare not, let go to drift into blessed sleep. It was all part of the job, and the many problems that arose had to be dealt with out of the reserve of strength which he had no idea existed.

February 1944 marked the pinnacle of Walker's triumphs in U-boat sinkings. In one operation, no less than six of the enemy were destroyed, a score unsurpassed by any other commanding officer in World War II. Such success was a reflection of his genius and obsession.

By June 1943, the balance of the Battle of the Atlantic had turned in the Allies' favour. During March, April, May and

June of that year, a total of 84 U-boats had been sunk by a joint effort of naval and air forces and by the end of the year that total had risen to 202. Such was this impact on the U-boat campaign that Doenitz was forced to withdraw the beaten remnants of his fleet from the Atlantic for a time and disperse them over other distant waters. And while Walker's groups were winning the Battle of the Atlantic, Allied merchant ships were being pursued and sunk in the South Atlantic and in American coastal waters.

In March 1941, the 9,000-ton freighter SS *Harlesden* left the Clyde for Halifax, Nova Scotia with sealed orders not to be opened until halfway across the Atlantic. By the 24th, the ship had reached a position 49 degrees north 43 degrees west and was some 500 miles east of Newfoundland. The seas running heavy, long between the crests, were being whipped up by a bitterly cold wind from the north-east. *Harlesden* was making heavy weather of it, her bows digging deep into the swell, with the seas running green over the foredeck. It was just after 11 a.m. that the wireless operator intercepted urgent calls from another ship in the area. The first message read 'Suspicious vessel sighted'. This was followed by 'Suspicious vessel closing'. Moments later came the dramatic and alarming signal 'Shelled'. That one laconic word was the last and probably the final transmission from a sinking freighter. In the mind of *Harlesden*'s Master, Captain C. Parry, it could mean only one thing; the unidentified ship in distress had been attacked by one of Germany's marauding heavy warships loose in the north Atlantic.

The possibility that it could be any one of four ships was frightening. Unconfirmed reports indicated that the two battle-cruisers *Gneisenau* and *Scharnhorst* and the two pocket-battleships *Lutzow* and *Scheer* had broken out and were attacking the trade routes between America and Britain. Even more frightening was the probability that the attacking warship was not far distant.

It was at precisely 1445 that Captain Parry heard the drone of an approaching aircraft, the reverberation of its pulsating engines growing louder and louder with every second that passed. The sound was from the skies to the north, with drifting clouds intermittently baffling the drone. Then at the same instant, he and the lookouts saw a lone plane streaking out of the clouds from about 5,000 feet holding a steady downward course straight for the ship. In that following fractional second, Parry realized it had to be an aircraft launched from a German warship. He already knew from his ship recognition book that *Lutzow* and *Scheer* each carried two aircraft and that *Gneisenau* and *Scharnhorst*, four.

Even as his hand slammed down on the 'Emergency Action Station' switch, the sound of the plane's engines rose to a crescendo. With its power dive steepening, it descended like a plummeting arrow straight for the *Harlesden*, the swastika symbol clearly visible on the wings and fuselage. Hardly had the strident scream of the warning klaxon died, than the DEMS gunners mounting the Hotchkiss anti-aircraft guns were pumping shells into the oncoming aircraft. At the gunnery school back home, grey-haired Royal Naval instructors, recalled for war service had in fact, never actually experienced enemy action. It was however their duty to convince their young conscripted pupils that a plane diving straight down on to a waiting, unflinching Hotchkiss gunner, never had a chance. That was the theory. In practice, a bomb-laden plane falling out of the sky in a near vertical dive at 400 miles an hour, with its ear-piercing wing scream and its guns discharging a stream of bullets, is one of the most frightening and difficult of all targets.

Nevertheless, despite the hail of bullets exploding all around, the *Harlesden* gunners resolutely held their ground, fingers locked around triggers. Pulling out of its dive seemingly just above mast height, two bombs floated out like large black Indian clubs, fins swaying, wobbling, whistling. They fell slowly at first, then faster and faster. One, scraping down the starboard side of the hull, lifted the ship from the force of the blast but the second was a direct hit, the starboard edge of the bridge taking the full force of the explosion. When the smoke cleared, the superstructure on that side gaped wide open.

Almost before the debris and dust settled, the aircraft had circled and was making a run-in for another attack, banking steeply to starboard, then swinging back to line-up on the ship. The concentrated fire from *Harlesden*'s guns, although scoring direct hits on the aircraft, seemed to have little effect for in a bid to avoid destruction it swerved, steadied, swerved again then roared in to swoop low over the freighter to drop another bomb barely missing the stern.

The third mate, William Mutimer, asleep in his cabin when the bomb landed was thrown out of his bunk by the force of the explosion. Rushing on deck, he saw the enemy plane turning to begin another attack. Climbing to the bridge, he discovered the second mate, David Souter, unconscious, lying face down, head split open, covered in blood. At this time, Captain Parry was in the wheelhouse (which was protected by concrete blocks) giving continuous change-of-course orders to the helmsman in order to dodge the bombs and the vicious machine-gun fire. Mutimer realized that Souter would have to be moved quickly, for he was lying in a position where he would be fully exposed to further machine-gun fire. Souter was a heavy man to move, but with the help of a young Swedish seaman, he tried to drag the man into the wheelhouse.

By now however, the aircraft was roaring down with its guns spitting a deadly stream of shells into the superstructure, and to save himself, the seaman threw himself into the wheelhouse, while Mutimer continued to try to drag Souter to safety. The concentration of bullets was tearing away plating and shattering debris in every direction, and it was at this instant that an iron bar, whirling through the air smashed into Mutimer's right arm, shattering the humerus, while another piece of metal cut into his right foot.

But Mutimer was not the only casualty, for that attack had killed or wounded all the deck officers leaving only the captain unhurt and able to keep watch. It was the aircraft's last raid and after another circuit around the ship it flew off northward. It was obvious that the plane must have been launched from a not too distant enemy ship. The significance of the morning's distress signal from the unknown vessel now increased the anxiety of the whole crew. They could only hope that under cover of darkness they might escape.

Bleeding profusely, Mutimer went below where the cook and the steward, who had received basic first-aid instructions, managed to put a splint on his arm and stem the flow of blood. At nine o'clock that night, the clear sound of several loud booms echoed across the sea. The duty gunner instinctively jumped to his feet with 'This is it, mate, bloody shells'. Two or three miles away white gouts of flame lanced out of the inky darkness, and a second later came the frightening roar, like that of an express train, followed by the mind-shattering noise like that of hundreds of dustbins flying around. As the heavy shells hit the hull of *Harlesden*, the ship shuddered under the impact, canting over with each blow.

As the minutes passed, with no pause in the explosions, the booms and flashes of the enemy guns grew nearer and with them the distinctive 'crack' of lighter guns, sharing in the bombardment. Damage was catastrophic. The side of *Harlesden* had been ripped out, the deck houses demolished and burning and most of the funnel torn away, with the after-mast scythed almost to the deck.

That *Harlesden* was finished there was little doubt, she was nothing more than a sinking burning hulk, and yet the bombardment went on and on in a sort of vengeful retaliation for the defence the freighter had put up against the earlier attacking aircraft. Shells continued to land on and around the ship with the explosions ripping away pieces of her decking and superstructure. Men were catapulted in all directions, into bone-breaking metal, dazed minds trying to reorientate themselves into a condition to survive. Suddenly the barrage stopped as though a giant hand had pulled a switch. On the ship, the crew in a confusion of shock, numbed minds, blasted eardrums, and stinging contracted throats from the effect of the acrid cordite fumes, stumbled and groped their way through the smoke to try to launch a lifeboat.

In the meantime, Mutimer, searching for his friend, found

him laid out unconscious in his cabin; with his own broken arm there was no way he could move him. To leave him there to drown was unthinkable and so, in a frenzy of despair, he raced out on deck to get help, only to find the ship partly submerged and rapidly sinking by the stern with the only lifeboat being quickly lowered. There was not a moment to lose and though in an agony of pain he managed to climb over the rail and throw himself into the boat. But the ship was still moving and as the lifeboat reached the water, it was almost pulled under with the sea sweeping over the bow. It was only by the quick release of the falls that they were saved from being capsized. As a result, at the release, the boat shot away from the side of the ship. Meanwhile, there were men hanging on the ship's rope ladders calling them to bring the lifeboat back. By rowing hard, every effort was made to close in and save them and to pick up others on rafts. But there were also many already in the sea swimming around in life-jackets with a battery-powered light glowing red in the darkness. By now *Harlesden* was sinking deeper and deeper. Hundreds of tons of water were rushing into the ship like a burst dam, racing through fractured and torn bulkheads, pulling the ship down and down. The poop-deck rails were already under water, the bows rising. For a brief moment the rescue operation paused, the rowers shipping their oars, the greedy, licking flames from the gaping holes in the hull and superstructure throwing an eerie light over the whole scene.

In the boat, tense white faces, eyes staring, watched in disbelief as their ship, their home, sank deeper into the black sea, hissing and spluttering in protest as the red-hot metal of the torn hull touched the cold Atlantic water. Even in the sea, many of the swimmers, black-faced with oil, turned momentarily to watch. For perhaps twenty seconds, *Harlesden* hung there, balanced between the sea and the blackness of the night sky, illuminated by the fires of her own destruction. As she started her last dive, there came a rending, tearing sound clear across the water, then suddenly she slid rapidly down – and was gone.

For the rescuers there was nothing left to do but to get on

with the job of rescue. For them it was a matter of rowing around in the darkness selecting the living from the dead, guided only by the shouting, pleading calls of the swimmers. Here and there amid the chorus of voices were the choking cries of men at the limit of their endurance, men without life-jackets who were to drown before they could be reached. The boat moved amidst the flotsam and jetsam and the black slurping fuel-oil spewed out in the ship's last moments, hauling inboard men in the last stages of exhaustion, searching until no more cries could be heard. All this time, unseen, the enemy vessel had been moving closer and closer.

Suddenly a glaring beam of light from the ship illuminated the whole area showing up the lifeboat and the drifting rafts. From the approaching ship, not more than one hundred yards away and closing, came a guttural voice ordering them to come alongside. Mutimer and the men in the boat, blinded by the dazzling light, could see nothing beyond the glare except a vague, ambiguous silhouette, menacing, featureless, black against the black sky. As they neared, several rope ladders and scrambling nets could be seen hanging from the ship's side. Mutimer realized that he with his broken arm would never be able to climb unaided and he shouted up, 'We have wounded men in the boat.'

First came those who could make it to the deck, shaking, trembling men, dressed in filthy, oil-sodden clothes, some with head wounds, others bare-armed and badly steam-scalded, men who stood in shocked silence, dumbfounded by the swiftness of the catastrophe, in wonderment at the solid deck on which they stood. At the same time, slings were thrown down while Mutimer and half-drowned and wounded men were hauled aboard: most silent, many coughing, retching up the poisonous fuel-oil that burned their lungs.

As Mutimer's legs hit the ship's side, he called out, 'Please don't touch my right arm'. Care was taken to do as he asked, and he was taken below into what appeared to be an operating theatre. The German officer who spoke excellent English then gave him an anaesthetic while his arm was reset and put in plaster. On awakening the officer informed him that he was now on board the famous battle cruiser *Gneisenau*. During the whole time he was on the ship, he was treated very well indeed, but after five days he was transferred to the supply ship *Ermland* and taken to occupied France. Unfortunately, some months later, his arm became gangrenous and had to be amputated. Despite this, his condition worsened, so much so that it was decided that only a blood transfusion could save him. Ironically, this was given by a young German orderly who laid beside him providing a direct man-to-man transfusion. From that day on his condition improved so much that he was finally transferred to a German prisoner-of-war camp. As William Mutimer later stated in his report: 'What a paradox, when one considers how all these people went to such lengths to save his life, when their countrymen had, in the first place done their best to kill him.' (*The Review* magazine, Naval Historical collectors and Research Association).

NOTE: Apart from the battleships *Tirpitz* and *Bismarck*, the battle-cruisers *Gneisenau* and *Scharnhorst* were the two most powerful warships ever built in Germany. Each of 32,000 tons, they had a steaming radius of 10,000 miles at 19 knots and a crew of 1,800. Their main armament comprised nine 11-inch, twelve 6-inch, fourteen 4-inch guns and fifty-four anti-aircraft guns, and they carried four aircraft. *Gneisenau*, in company with her sister ship *Scharnhorst*, became the pirates of the North Atlantic, sinking twenty-two ships totalling 115,622 tons.

A further illustration of Doenitz's decision to extend his U-boats' activities into American coastal waters is revealed with the story of the freighter the SS *Cyclops* of 9,700 tons. On 2 January 1942, *Cyclops* left Cristobal in Venezuela with a general cargo heading for Halifax, Nova Scotia. The crew numbered 103, made up of Europeans and Chinese; in addition, 78 Chinese passengers made a total of 181 persons aboard.

Cyclops had originally set out from Hong Kong and having

passed through the Panama Canal and calling in at Cristobal, sailed north for Halifax. By 11 January, having covered a voyage of approximately 14,000 miles and reached a position 41 degrees 51 north, 63 degrees 48 west, she was only 200 miles from her destination. The previous night, her master, Captain L.R. Kersley, had received a signal warning him that German submarines were believed operating in that area and as a consequence of that information he had been zigzagging the ship until darkness fell, intending to re-commence the pattern at 8 p.m.

The ship was sailing independent, in other words without the protection of an armed escort, not that an accompanying destroyer or corvette could ensure immunity from an enemy torpedo. But it was always a comfort to have the company of another ship in case that frightening nightmare might become a reality. Captain Kersley was fully aware that out of their long voyage, this last 200 miles might be the most dangerous. In ports on both sides of the Atlantic, masters of freighters had often privately discussed the possibility of Admiral Doenitz extending his U-boat activities from mid-Atlantic to the easier and richer pickings of American coastal waters.

This premise proved correct, for at the end of 1941, Doenitz, realizing how less hazardous it would be for his boats to sink ships off the American coast, launched 'Operation Paukenschlag' (Drumroll) consisting of a fleet of twenty-four large ocean-going submarines. The first five, U.123, U.130, U.66, U.109 and U.125, were all large type IXB boats of 1100 tons, armed with one 4.1 gun and two smaller anti-aircraft guns and having a complement of 48 men. These boats reached their hunting grounds on 11 January 1942, the day that *Cyclops* arrived in the area, and in the following four weeks they sank twenty-six Allied merchant ships totalling 163,021 tons. But *Cyclops* was the first to fall victim, and that to U.123. Her Commanding Officer, Korvetten Kapitan Hardegen, was by far the most successful U-boat captain of Operation Paukenschlag, sinking nine ships totalling 53,173 tons.

On his return to Lorient, Hardegen was awarded the

Knight's Cross and promoted to Freggatenkapitan. Both he and U.123 survived the war but the other four boats were all sunk by Allied offensive action.

U.130	12 March 1943	West of Azores by USN destroyer *Champlin*
U.66	6 May 1944	Off Cape Verde by aircraft from USN escort carrier *Black Island* and destroyer *Buckley*
U.125	6 May 1943	Off Newfoundland by RN destroyer *Vidette*
U.109	7 May 1943	Off Southern Ireland by British aircraft

As *Cyclops* sailed north that night, a cold wind was blowing with steady determination out of the north-west. A wind that forced deck crewmen to bury their faces deeper into coat collars and lower their heads for protection. A resolute wind, lifting the Atlantic sea into a heavy swell, long between the crests, each with a fleck of white along its ridge. *Cyclops* was already dipping her prow with heavy spray bursting high over the port bow, there to be snatched away by the wind to drench the forward hatches. To say it was dark was an understatement; it was very dark, no moon – not even a cloud-coated moon – and the stars had long hidden their light. Although Admiralty merchant ships had been given instructions that dimmed navigation lights were to be shown in American waters, Kersley decided to ignore the order in the interest of safety.

But on that never-to-be-forgotten night of 11 January, waiting in the path of *Cyclops*' northward advance, lay U.123. The commanding officer, Kapitan Hardegen, had stationed his boat astride the trade route between Florida and Novia Scotia. At 7 p.m. that evening, his hydrophones picked up the sound of an approaching ship, and sounding 'Action stations', he dived to periscope depth, waited and watched. How he could have distinguished the shape of a ship in that darkness was a mystery. Nevertheless, dimly framed against the darkness, there emerged the sheer huge bulk of a freighter. After many hours of inaction here was the opportunity he and the crew had been waiting for. Swinging the periscope around, he checked for the possible presence of other ships but there was nothing, no freighters, no warship escorts, nothing, just a lone cargo vessel plodding along at a steady fifteen knots. U.123 was now slightly ahead of its quarry and moving in on an interception course. Eyes glued to the 'scope he began the run in, checking the target distance. The crew, tense, silent, expectant, hands on controls, watched the captain's face, awaiting orders.

In a calm, steady voice, the commands came clear, precise: 'Flood torpedo tubes one and two.'

Five seconds later with the distance closing: 'Steady as you go.'

Without moving his eyes from the 'scope he gave the next order: 'Open bow caps. Enemy course 12. Bow left. Range 600, torpedo speed 40.'

The executive officer confirmed with: 'Tubes ready for firing.'

It was the 'now' moment. Crisply came the execute order. 'Fire one.'

The boat shuddered with a muffled vibration. As the torpedo burst from its bow tube, it sped on towards the doomed ship with 750 lbs of Amatol in its warhead.

At this distance Hardegen estimated a twenty-five second run to target. Beside him, the armament officer, stop watch in hand, read off the seconds. Within the boat there hung a silence as heavy as the thick stagnant air that pervaded every compartment. An unreal scene with the crew transfixed into statuesque immobility, as though caught by the instant shutter of a camera, standing, sitting, crouching, unblinking, straining to catch the report of the torpedo strike. At twenty-eight seconds Hardegen cursed, thinking the torpedo had missed. An instant later came the sound they had all been waiting for – one loud booming explosion. He withheld the firing of tube No. 2, awhile.

So distant from the U-boat base at Brest, he would need to conserve his stock of torpedoes. It was always possible that the one already fired would sink the ship anyway. Unseen,

U.123 surfaced like a dripping monster and then in the darkness, from the conning tower, Hardegen watched the sinking ship.

When the torpedo struck *Cyclops* it was exactly 7.45 p.m. It entered the starboard side, ploughed through the hull and exploded between No. 6 and 7 hatches and just abaft the engine room. Under the enormous hammer blow of the explosion, the 9,000-ton freighter lurched to port, slewing around crazily. While the damage was catastrophic, it was further compounded by the ship's 15-knot speed. Below and above decks, passengers and crew were hurled this way and that under the impact. The blast shattered the stillness of the night lighting the darkness with a single beacon of flame shooting skyward.

In the wireless office, the senior radio officer, R.P. Morrison, was almost flung from his chair. Above him, the switchboards were wrenched from the securing bolts causing some damage but not enough to stop transmission. At the instant, Morrison flashed a distress call, constantly repeating it; then running out on to the boat deck he checked that lifeboat no. 4 on the port side had its portable emergency transmitter and receiver aboard. By now the ship was sinking by the stern, and with another dash back to the office he rebroadcast the call several times until receiving a reply from V.C.S. Camperdown, confirming receipt.

There was nothing more he could do and on Captain Kersley's orders he ran forward and stood by the port raft. Below decks and in every compartment forward and aft, everything was in a state of chaos. Beds and bunks, tables and crockery, chairs and stools, all battered and smashed, were scattered in every direction, and amidst this tangled miscellany of sliding, heaving wreckage, scores of shouting, frightened Chinese passengers and crew fought and struggled to reach the upper deck and the boats.

From the moment the torpedo struck, Kersley moved swiftly into action. Already the stern-rails were dipping, and while the ship could not be saved, his responsibility lay in saving the lives of the 181 people aboard. With the help of

Senior Midshipman Desmond Stewart, they managed to get five boats away, but in the panic that ensued many Chinese lost their lives in the rush to secure places in the boats.

On the starboard side, while boat no. 3 was being lowered filled with Chinese, and while the ship still had considerable way on her, the forward fall slipped, upending the boat, throwing the occupants into the sea, leaving it pendant, swinging. Underneath it, thrashing about in the water were some forty or fifty men, shouting, screaming, waving their arms, pleading to be saved. But the hanging boat had to be launched. With many men still crowding the rails and the ship sinking, every available craft, every raft, every floatable object was absolutely crucial to survival. In a desperate bid to save the whaler, one of the junior officers cut the after fall. From some fifty feet the boat plummeted down on to the mass of swimmers below. Across the deck on the port side, boats nos. 4 and 6 were also in trouble. As both were being lowered, one of the life-lines became foul, drawing no. 4 back against the hull. As it reached the water, the heaving swell caught the bow, smashing into no. 6 boat close by, causing severe damage.

From the U-boat's conning tower, Hardegen studied the scene with some disquiet. True, the freighter's stern was low in the water, but many a torpedoed ship had been made salvable by a timely and effective operation. He decided that not only would she have to be sunk but be seen to have been sunk. By this time, *Cyclops* had slewed around and was now showing her starboard hull. For the U-boat captain it was the ideal position to apply the 'coup de grace'. Intercom in hand, he quietly gave the order 'Fire two.'

It was at about this moment that Captain Kersley, having collected the ship's papers and crossing to the port side of the bridge, heard the sharp urgent shout from one of his officers, 'Look out, it's another torpedo.' It was undoubtedly this warning and Kersley's agile leap that saved him. The torpedo struck the hull underneath the bridge immediately below where he had been standing, hurling a sheet of flame and flying debris mast high. The swift action in throwing himself backward unquestionably saved his life. This second torpedo was the death blow. Below deck, the mass of water rushing into the ship tore away bulkheads, destroying everything in its path. In the engine-room, Second Engineer McDavid was on watch when the second torpedo struck, yet, despite his awareness that the ship would go down in a matter of minutes, he remained at his post until the last moment. That moment came when he saw the far bulkhead split open and a wall of water come pounding towards him.

In desperation he raced for the ladder, but was waist deep before his hand grasped the top rung, with the water sucking greedily at his legs to drag him back. As he looked down at the swirling torrent that had so nearly trapped him, he could see a single light burning under water glowing through the dark green vortex. Shuddering, he threw himself clear and raced up and out into the cold night air, where the canting deck told him he had only minutes to save himself.

Meanwhile Captain Kersley and Midshipman Stewart were struggling against the sloping deck, trying to reach and cut the rafts adrift. Under their feet the ship was sinking deeper and deeper, the bow steadily lifting. Around other parts of the ship men were sliding and slipping, cursing wildly, clutching at anything and everything to save themselves from tumbling downward on to steel projections. Above their heads, the steam safety valve was emitting a piercing whistle, rising higher and higher, drowning shouted orders and the babel of terrified Chinese. In the darkness, Kersley and Stewart were just able to follow the line of the ship. Beneath them, nothing but a steep slope that led nowhere except into the sea. On the starboard side, Fourth Officer Tom Haverfield managed to lift the shocked-stunned third officer over the side into the water and pull him on to a nearby raft. Fifty yards away, one of the Chinese passengers, struggling to keep afloat, screamed for help. Without hesitation, Haverfield turned back, reached the man and towed him to the raft where he was pulled aboard. Unfortunately, only two hours later the Chinaman died. By now, the ship was only moments away from her final plunge, clearly signalled by a violent lurch.

While the bows rose higher still, the deck-rails were crowded with those who had failed to reach the boats and it was here that fear took hold. In the confused hullabaloo of Chinese trying to raise their voices above the strident scream of the steam safety-valve, many jumped into the sea and struck out from the ship, panting and gasping with the intensity of the cold. Others clinging to the rails tried to climb higher towards the rising bows but with their strength failing, they fell back into the water. Just before *Cyclops'* last moment, when only the bow hung above the sea, two men remained on board, Midshipman Stewart and Captain Kersley.

With the rafts now cut free, Stewart swam away to one of these followed by the captain. The time was 8 p.m. It seemed almost impossible to believe that only fifteen minutes had elapsed since the first torpedo struck. As they reached the rafts, *Cyclops'* prow rose almost vertical, then with a certain finality, the ship slid down and down. As the tip of the bows disappeared, a mass of turbulent water leapt upwards and with it came the pungent smell of oil.

A history of thirty-six sea years had been wiped out in a matter of fifteen war minutes. Even in summer, the waters of the North Atlantic can fairly be described as cold, in winter it is near to freezing, and it was into this bitter element that those who had survived the explosions and who took to the water, to the rafts or the boats, found themselves. The boat people had the best of it, but for the rest it was sheer hell. Such was the sea swell that even those on the rafts were awash most of the time.

For those left in the water, death came within the hour, the cold not only numbing the senses but shutting off the vital blood flow to the heart. Throughout that long, neverending night and the long forenoon and afternoon of the next day, several men on the rafts, lapsing into unconsciousness, slid off and drifted away. The worst fatalities were in the boats filled with Chinese, where, unused to the colder climes of the northern hemisphere, exposure took a heavy toll.

Late that afternoon, a Catalina flying boat sighted them

and, after flying around for a while, flew off to direct the HMCS *Red Deer* to their assistance. In the first two boats that *Red Deer* came upon, filled with Chinese, only one man was left alive. In the other boats also, deaths from exposure were mainly among the Chinese. In his report, Captain Kersley recounts that on his raft only five, including the midshipman were left alive. He states: 'I consider that within another two hours we should all have been dead owing to the extreme cold.'

In naming several of his crew for their courage and fortitude, Kersley particularly commends Desmond Stewart who stayed with him throughout until the ship went down, cutting the rafts free and using great intelligence and initiative. He ascribes the utmost praise to Second Engineer McDavid for his gallantry in staying at his post in the engine-room to the last moment. Unfortunately, McDavid, who came up from the hot engine-room dressed only in a thin boiler suit, was one of those who died from exposure on a raft. In the final roll-call, out of the 181 crew and passengers aboard, 88 perished.

Note: SS *Cyclops*, built at Glasgow in 1906, was one of six ships constructed for the firm of Holt & Co, better known as the Blue Funnel line; the six being *Cyclops, Teucea, Titan, Antilochus, Bellerophon* and *Protesilaus*, all these following the tradition of ship names taken from Greek mythology. Interestingly, in January 1917, in the Great War, *Cyclops* survived a submarine attack. Ironically, her next U-boat encounter was in January 1942.

In World War II, in January 1940, she served as a combined infantry and landing-craft ship for combined operations in Norway at Narvik. When this operation came to an end, *Cyclops* was dispatched to Brest with her sister ships to take part in Operation Aerial, the rescue of troops from western France. After service in the Pacific in 1941, she departed for Cristobal on 2 January for Halifax, Nova Scotia, where she was sunk by U-boat 123, with the loss of many lives.

Citations

Citation for Lloyd's War Medal for Bravery at Sea which appeared in Lloyd's List and Shipping Gazette of Friday, 1 January 1943.

Desmond Hamilton Stewart, Midshipman
Cyclops

The ship was badly damaged by an enemy submarine and, later, sank. Midshipman Stewart showed courage and resource throughout, particularly in the launching of boats, and in helping to cut the lashings and free the forward rafts. He stayed on board until the end, only leaving before the Master, after being ordered to do so. He also set a fine example to others on the raft.

Kings Commendation for Brave Conduct, *London Gazette* 23/6/42.

1 Captain Leslie Webber Kersley.
2 Second Engineer Officer Gordon Scott McDavid (Posthumous)
3 Midshipman Desmond Hamilton Stewart, RNR.

Desmond Stewart was commissioned as Temp Sub Lt. RNR 29/3/43, and on 2 August that year was appointed to HMS *Findhorn*. He served on for the remainder of the war in the Atlantic, the Indian Ocean (involved in sinking of U.198 on 8 August 1944) and Central Pacific with British Task Force as part of the escort for the British Supply Group. After the war he returned to Alfred Holt & Co and in 1946 continued his career with that company being appointed Master in the late 1950s. Concurrently with this, he advanced through the RNR, eventually reaching Flag Rank, a great achievement, as there are only ever two RNR men serving at one time with that rank. In honour of that achievement, he was appointed an Additional Commander of the Military Division of the Most Excellent Order of the

British Empire in the Birthday Honours of 12 June 1976.

These foregoing examples of Doenitz's extended campaign into American waters are but two of many such events, events brought about by the German admiral's humiliation in being temporarily driven out of his Atlantic hunting grounds by Captain Johnny Walker's escort group's victories over the U-boat in the Central Atlantic. The single-minded purpose to seek, to find and destroy the enemy, was perpetuated by his amazing energy to remain on the bridge for long hours despite punishing fatigue, refusing to surrender to nature's demand for sleep.

By February 1944, this dedication to duty was making greater demands on his strength. Not immediately apparent was a latent deterioration. His latest and overwhelming victory in the destruction of six U-boats in one patrol caught the imagination of the press and the British public. Captain Johnny Walker became the nation's hero. On the group escort's return to Liverpool he received the congratulations of the Prime Minister Winston Churchill, the Chiefs of the War Cabinet and the Admiralty on the success of the ships under his command. Their arrival proved a pageantry of welcome where almost 2,000 naval and dockyard personnel cheered and waved to greet them. In World War II history books, Johnny Walker is described as Britain's most outstanding U-boat killer, responsible for the sinking of twenty submarines. It was a triumphal home-coming, for no hunting group had ever inflicted such punishment upon Admiral Doenitz's much lauded submarine fleet. As a result of these astonishing achievements a grateful Admiralty awarded him his fourth DSO.

But by now, such had been the demands of duties at sea, that the crews of the entire escort group were at the limit of their endurance. This was evident in Walker's case, although to his crews he was careful to present a cheerful, optimistic front. The blow fell when he was suddenly taken ill and rushed to the Royal Naval Hospital at Seaforth. The long months and years of unswerving devotion to the Royal Navy in discharging his responsibility, even beyond the call of duty, had taken its toll. Two days later on 9 July 1944 he died from cerebral thrombosis. The news of his death came not only as a great shock to the Second Support group who admired and revered him but also to the whole nation. The funeral service held at Liverpool Cathedral was attended by an estimated thousand people, who came to pay their silent tribute to a valiant leader who had played a major role in making the seas safe for Allied Merchant ships and their crews – the man they affectionately knew as Captain Johnny Walker, RN.

While Doenitz may have breathed a momentary sigh of relief at the demise of his adversary, the days of the U-boat campaign in the Atlantic and indeed elsewhere were numbered, for the strategy which Captain Walker had introduced and which had proved so rewarding was sustained by all other escort groups. In the face of these adversities and while defeat stared him in the face, he refused to acknowledge that the effectiveness of the Allied successes against his U-boats was the cumulative result of superior tactics, better weapons and the cooperation of surface and air escorts. Never did he accept that he had been worsted or outmanoeuvred, but there is little doubt that his U-boat empire started to crumble when Captain John Walker went to sea and challenged him on the waters of the Atlantic.

Stung by growing defeats, Doenitz intensified his efforts to sink merchant ships and it was to be many months before the scourge of the U-boats was erased from the oceans. Even as late as 1944, he had an average of 170 U-boats ready for or actually operating, and a further 300 undergoing training and sea trials. This was in addition to 360 completed or nearing completion in the dockyads and a further 1,470 on the drawing board. No wonder Winston Churchill in his memoirs was prompted to say – 'The only thing that ever really frightened me during the war was the U-boat peril.'

Ever the optimist, Doenitz maintained that the heavy destruction of his U-boats and their crews, which included that of his own son, was justified by his steadfast appreciation that the U-boat was the only weapon in German warfare that could have won the war, and that even in 1943, it constituted the only remaining means of effective offensive warfare.

8 The Merchant Ship – The MV *Hopetarn*

When anti-submarine measures in the Atlantic became increasingly effective, Doenitz struck some well-timed blows at unprotected shipping in less dangerous waters such as the Cape, the West Indies and the Indian Ocean. He reasoned that since the Allied Command had announced their policy of 'unconditional surrender', he could do no more than make things as uncomfortable as possible for them, by never relaxing the threat to their shipping.

In this context, the account of the fate of the merchant vessel *Hopetarn* is a typical example. Most of the crew of the freighter were cheerful enough as they set out on the 5,000-mile voyage from Colombo, Ceylon, to Durban, South Africa. Although the sea was fairly rough, lifting from a southerly Force 5, visibility was good and the skies reasonably clear. Sailing independently without protective escort however, had prompted one or two to voice their fears but this mood of despondency had been rapidly dispelled by the buoyant spirit of the others, who were quick to point out that here in the vast area of the Indian Ocean, the chances of being torpedoed were minimal. After all, they argued, the massive submarine warfare being fought by Hitler was concentrated in the North Atlantic and Arctic convoy routes. It was true that a few U-boats and even a German surface raider had strayed into the South Atlantic, but here in this great expanse of sea it would be difficult for the enemy to operate with such long lines of supply and communication, being 8,000 miles from their nearest base.

The *Hopetarn* of 5,230 tons, was loaded with 9,000 tons of general cargo and among its crew of forty-four were four naval and four army gunners manning the ship's armament of ten guns. Fourteen days later, they were on the last leg of their voyage with about 200 miles to go. Just after seven o'clock that evening, the master of the vessel, Captain Wilson, was startled to hear a loud thud on the port side, as though something had struck the ship. He at once dispatched the chief officer with the carpenter to make a thorough search of every department. It sounded as if it might have been a torpedo striking the hull with its warhead failing to explode. Despite the search, nothing was discovered, and the vessel appeared to be in good trim.

All this time, their course had been southward but now, with Durban on their starboard beam, Captain Wilson altered course to west. Forty-five minutes later, when in position 31 degrees south, 40 degrees east, and in darkness, the ship shuddered under the enormous impact of a torpedo from a submerged U-boat. It plunged into the engine-room on the starboard side, tearing away a large section of the hull. The explosion was tremendous, with flames shooting out of the engine-room skylight to a height of 150 feet. Like the bursting of a dam, tons of water poured into the vessel, yet, despite the improbability of survival, all the stokers and engineers managed to reach the ladders and escape through the hatchways. On deck the explosion had created a disaster area; the main mast had collapsed, the starboard accommodation was blown away, the two starboard lifeboats and part of the bridgehouse and all lights and electrical power utterly destroyed.

Recovering from the effects of the explosion, Captain Wilson ordered the chief officer to prepare the boats for lowering and instructed the third officer to muster all hands on deck. By now the ship was settling quickly and it was clear there was little time. Meeting with the wireless officer, he ordered him to transmit a distress call, but he reported that this had been found impossible as the transmission set had been put out of action. Wilson had some doubts about this and returned with the operator to the wireless room, as it was vital that a distress call should be dispatched but one glance was sufficient to confirm the story – the wireless room was a complete shambles. No more could be done and the order was given to 'abandon ship'.

A bright starlit night gave some light, and returning to the boat deck, he found some of the crew trying to lower the two port lifeboats but this was proving difficult as both boats were jammed by debris. Turning his attention to the small boat on the port side, with the help of two seamen, he managed to get the lashings off and lowered it into the water. One of the seamen who helped to lower the boat climbed down the ladder, but when within reachable distance someone cut the painter and the boat drifted away. In trying to jump into the boat he missed it and fell, but was quickly rescued.

The rest of the crew were still having difficulty in clearing the debris from the lifeboats. Eventually, the wreckage fouling them was cleared and as many men as possible were put into the larger boat with the second officer in charge and lowered into the water. This now left three seamen, the carpenter, chief engineer, first officer and the captain aboard.

Whilst this was going on, one of the naval gunners commenced climbing down the ladder but when halfway, he lost his footing, slipped, appeared to strike his head on the ship's side as he fell between the ship and the lifeboat and was not seen again. In the meantime, on an adjacent ladder, two seamen, when halfway down, took fright and clung to the rungs, refusing either to jump into the boat or climb back on board. The men already in the lifeboat reached out to try to pull them in but were unable to do so and later they went down with the ship.

The vessel was listing 45 degrees to starboard; it then gave a sudden lurch, and Wilson, thinking she was about to turn over, gave orders for the lifeboat to pull clear, shouting to the men still on board to jump for it, whilst he ran down the ship's side into the water. Dreading the thought of being sucked down, he swam frantically towards the lifeboat and was hauled aboard. Looking back, he saw that the after-deck of the *Hopetarn*, from stern to funnel, was now completely under water, the bow rising higher and higher as she poised ready for the last downward plunge. As the tilting increased, there came the crash of shifting cargo, the rending of tearing metal and the roar of explosions from somewhere deep in the bowels of the ship as trapped steam and air burst through the bulkheads and hatches.

Five minutes later, in a great pool of foaming bubbles, oil and debris, her end came suddenly, rising vertically to plunge swiftly to the bottom. As *Hopetarn* sank, the enormous suction drew the lifeboat over the top of the vortex and instinctively everyone clung to the sides, expecting to be drawn under but even as the boat began to be sucked lower and lower, there was a sudden rush of air from the ship, lifting and thrusting it away from the danger zone.

There were obviously men in the water, for not too far away they could see red torch lights attached to lifejackets, and they started to pull in that direction. However, before they could reach the swimmers, a German U-boat surfaced about 200 yards away and for a moment it seemed about to ram them. Everyone in the boat shouted frantically, flashing their torches. Then from the submarine a voice shouted, 'Put out those lights'. This done, an order was given to pull the boat alongside. This proved difficult, as the lifeboat was hemmed in by cases of cargo floating around. The voice from the submarine, now impatient, shouted, 'Unless you obey our order immediately we shall open fire'. Eventually they managed to get clear, leaving the other boat to pick up the swimmers. As they approached, the voice called, 'What ship?', to which the men replied '*Hopetarn*'. Then came the question, 'Is the Captain there?' Although nothing had been arranged beforehand, all the men shouted: 'No, he's gone down with the ship.'

'Are you British?'

'Yes.'

'Good,' said the voice.

'Are you white?'

'Yes, all of us.'

'Very good,' came the reply.

'Any more ships?'

'No, no more.'

'Then that is a great pity.'

By now, the boat was alongside and the order was given for one man to come aboard. Wilson stepped on to the narrow deck and as he did so, he noticed four men standing close by, armed with machine-guns, wearing only singlets and trousers.

The submarine was about 250 feet long and, with its freshly painted coat of light grey, appeared to have recently come out of dry dock. The conning tower was oval-shaped with a platform at one end and jumping wires rigged fore and aft. Behind the conning tower, there appeared to be a 3-inch dual-purpose gun with a larger gun on the forward decking. Wilson was then conducted down the conning tower to a small cabin where he was interviewed by an officer. A smallish man, slightly bald with fair hair turning grey, bushy eyebrowed, thick-necked and stockily built with a pronounced Roman nose.

It was difficult to determine if he was the commander of the boat or not, as he was dressed in a field-grey uniform with twisted braid epaulets on the shoulder and seemed to be rather an officer of the German Army. He spoke quite good English but seemed arrogant and impatient and continually shook his finger threateningly. He looked Wilson up and down, then said: 'I have a number of questions to ask which you will answer correctly, otherwise I warn you, it will not go well for you and your friends; firstly the name of the ship?'

'*Hopetarn*, as we have already told you,' replied Wilson.

A flash of anger appeared in the German's eyes, then he asked, 'And what cargo were you carrying?'

'A general miscellaneous cargo of about 9000 tons.'

'Any explosives or war equipment?'

'No.'

The keen eyes carefully studied Wilson's face as he asked the next question. 'And what are you aboard this ship?'

It was a question loaded with danger for if he admitted that he was the captain, he would almost certainly be kept aboard and eventually be sent to a prisoner-of-war camp.

In any case, his men in the lifeboat had already lied to protect him by saying that their captain had gone down with the ship; he had to maintain the deception.

'I'm just an ordinary seaman,' replied Wilson.

'In that case,' said the German suspiciously, 'why did you come on board first and not one of the officers?'

'Well,' said Wilson, 'you were very impatient and as the bows of the boat, where I was, came up against the submarine first, I decided to step aboard.'

It was difficult to determine if the officer was convinced or not, but there was a flicker of a smile in the grey eyes. If he guessed, the matter was not pursued. He then produced a large book in which were recorded owners' names and a list of their ships. He studied this for some time then shouted angrily, 'You are lying to me, the *Hopetarn* is not listed here. I put it to you that your vessel was the *Hopestar*, not the *Hopetarn*?'

'I assure you,' replied Wilson resolutely, 'that our ship was the *Hopetarn*. I have no reason to lie.'

At first the German refused to believe him, until a junior officer nearby produced a smaller book in which the *Hopetarn* was indeed recorded. Wilson was then shown a silhouette of the *Hopestar* and asked if this was the type of ship which had been sunk, to which he replied, 'No, that is a steamship, the *Hopetarn* was a motor vessel.' The book seemed to have a list of all British ships belonging to various companies with the silhouette of each ship appearing at the head of the company's name.

'My information is that you were bound for Durban,' said the German. To this Wilson made no reply.

'Before you abandoned ship,' continued the officer, 'did you manage to transmit a distress call?'

'That I do not know. I was not near the wireless room at the time and did not know what orders were given.'

'How many men are in your lifeboats?'

'I'm not sure,' replied Wilson, 'but there are a number missing which we shall have no hope of saving.'

The German shrugged his shoulders. 'It is war and this is the price of war.'

'Yes, I know,' replied Wilson, 'I quite realize it is war but ...' Before he could finish, the German interrupted him.

'Yes, it is war, your war, a war you are fighting for Churchill, for Roosevelt, for the rich man and the Jew, and now for the Bolsheviks. My advice to you is that if you ever reach land safely, don't go back to sea.'

'But,' said Wilson, 'I have been to sea for over twenty years and there is nothing else I could do.'

'Ah, then you have been at sea about the same time as myself; however, you may not be so lucky next time.'

During this interrogation, the officer gave an order in German and what appeared to be a portable 'T' aerial, about six feet in height with a thick wire connecting it to one of the compartments, was passed through into the conning tower.

The German now seemed to adopt a friendlier attitude. 'Have a drink, it will warm you.' Another officer, behind Wilson, then came forward with a small tot of brandy which he accepted.

'There is one more question,' said the German, 'have you a transmitter on board?'

Wilson was not sure if he meant in the lifeboat or on board the ship, so playing for safety, he replied, 'No, it was destroyed in the explosion.'

The German nodded, then smiled. 'Very well, you can go back to your boat now and "Good luck".'

A crew member then showed him the way back to the lifeboat, but as he reached the deck and started walking towards the stern, one of the crew began punching him in the ribs. Wilson thought they were trying to rouse his temper, but suddenly realized they were at the same time bringing the second officer on board and did not want the two men to meet. However, as they passed, he managed to whisper, 'Say as little as possible,' then went aft and got into the boat. The second officer was absent for only two or three minutes; at the end of which time he was allowed to return, and having been asked the same questions, admitted to being the second officer and in charge of the lifeboat.

Having told him they were 200 miles from the nearest landfall, the U-boat steamed away on the surface. A little later, still in darkness, the submarine returned, having sighted the small port lifeboat with six men in it, including the third officer, and ordered it alongside. There was some commotion in this operation, as in trying to get aboard, the third officer accidentally kicked out the plug and the boat rapidly started to fill. Having climbed on to the deck of the submarine, he tried to explain their predicament to one of the German crew and asked if all the men could be brought aboard but they ignored him and pushed him along into the conning tower where he was also questioned.

Meantime, the crew in the lifeboat had fortunately found and replaced the plug and were able to bale out and save the boat. The German officer seemed satisfied with the answers received and minutes later the third officer was allowed to return. The U-boat then sped away but as she did so, the stern swung round, caught the side of the boat and capsized it, throwing everyone into the water. Cold and shivering, they eventually managed to haul themselves back into the boat which had fortunately righted itself.

An hour later, the silhouette of the submarine was seen again quite near. Twice it passed by, apparently without seeing them, and Wilson ordered the crew to unship their oars and keep quiet, but on passing a third time, they were sighted and again ordered back alongside. By this time Wilson had taken charge of the boat and was at the tiller. Reasonably, the second officer pointed out that if they saw him at the tiller, they would know he was not an ordinary seaman, so they changed places. As they drew near, the officer stood up and shone the torch on himself, while the crew shouted, 'Same boat'.

Again the second officer was ordered to come aboard and as he reached the conning tower, the submarine without any warning, steamed off at full speed, dragging the lifeboat along with it. This action pulled the boat partly up on to the hull and with the build up of the turbulence from the increased speed, the lifeboat again capsized. Even as it was beginning to turn over, someone had the presence of mind to cut the line and to set the boat free, into which they again had to climb. But by this time, the submarine had disappeared, taking the second officer with her, and he was not seen again.

It was still several hours to dawn and they searched the area thoroughly, shining their torches and shouting, but no survivors were found. By now, a strong wind had begun to blow; water was lopping into the boat and, almost to a man, everyone was violently seasick.

Originally, the lifeboat's wireless transmitting set had been left behind, but in the last few moments before *Hopetarn* had sunk, Wilson remembered it, and the young apprentice J.G. Wilson volunteered to return to the ship for it if someone else would come with him. In the event, the second radio officer John Moore offered to go with him and although the ship was listing heavily and in danger of sinking at any moment, they returned on board and collected both the transmitting and receiving sets. It was this brave act which eventually led to their rescue.

Although the temptation was strong, Wilson decided not to send out a distress call that night, as he considered the submarine might still be in the vicinity and would easily intercept it. So, with the small boat in tow and the sail hoisted, he set course for land, steering haphazardly by the stars. The following morning, as dawn lit the sky, the submarine was nowhere to be seen and with the wireless aerial rigged, they transmitted a distress signal, calling on any ship in the area to come to their aid. They gave the approximate position, stating there were two boats containing survivors from the *Hopetarn*. Twice more that day they transmitted but received no reply, and although the battery was practically new and in perfect working condition, they were determined to conserve battery power for as long as possible.

On the afternoon of the 31st, one of the men sighted smoke on the horizon. As it neared, the masts and funnel of a ship came into view. They then transmitted another message, 'British ship, two lifeboats on your starboard beam'. But it was obvious they had not been seen as no message was received, so estimating the vessel's course, Wilson steered to cut across it with the men rowing as hard as possible, but still the ship made no move in their direction. He then hoisted the big yellow flag to the top of the aerial mast and transmitted another message, 'Search on your starboard beam, two lifeboats, survivors on board, one boat flying yellow flag.'

It was this second message which brought identification, for one of the crew of the steamship climbed the foremast with binoculars and sighted them. Within an hour, the vessel was close enough to be identified as the SS *Nirvana*. By four o'clock that afternoon, after nearly two days, all the occupants of the large lifeboat numbering twenty-six were taken aboard and twenty minutes later the small boat with six was picked up.

Out of the total crew of the *Hopetarn*, twelve men were missing, but it seemed that but for the recovery of the wireless equipment many more lives would have been lost. Four days later, on 3 June, the *Nirvana* arrived with its party of survivors at the port of Durban.

9   The MV *Shillong*

In World War II, as soon as survivors from sunken merchant ships arrived back in port, it was an essential requirement to have a debriefing session immediately in order to obtain every scrap of information possible, while the details of their often tragic experiences were fresh in their minds. Fortunately, these records have been preserved in the archives of maritime history as a sober reminder not only of the hardship and suffering which had to be endured but also of the courage of the men of the merchant service who had to face Hitler's forces and fight back with all their vigour, not only to survive but also to defeat the objective of the enemy to annihilate them.

The story of the *Shillong* is but one of many in the long saga of merchant ships destroyed in the Battle of the Atlantic but it holds a pride of place in these records of human endurance and valour.

In April 1943, the motor vessel *Shillong* was the leading ship in a convoy bound from New York to Liverpool. Not even the duty lookouts saw the track of the deadly torpedo speeding directly towards them. Dead on target, the long, steel fish with its killer warhead streaked relentlessly towards its victim, the 5000 ton freighter, and there, on the port side, it crashed through the steel plating into the engine-room to explode in a holocaust of death and destruction.

A huge column of water, some fifty feet high was thrown

up, all lights went out, the chartroom and wheelhouse collapsed, practically every door was blown off its hinges and, unhappily, wireless equipment was destroyed, making it impossible to transmit a distress call. The time 10.15 p.m.

The *Shillong* had left New York, carrying a cargo of 9,000 tons of zinc concentrates and 2,000 tons of grain, stores urgently needed in the UK, fighting to maintain its pipeline of supplies from the United States. Markedly vulnerable to torpedo attacks from U-boats at this period, our merchant fleet vessels were being sunk at the rate of thousands of tons per week. Of the *Shillong*'s crew of seventy-eight, there were nine gunners manning anti-aircraft and anti-submarine guns. In practical terms, the latter were useless, as few U-boats ever surfaced to reveal their position until torpedoes had plunged into the target, leaving the ship in a sinking condition.

On that night of 4 April, as the sound of the explosion died away, the *Shillong* listed to port and slowly began to sink by the bow. In the total darkness, the effect was terrifying. Those who had not been killed by the explosion rushed to the boats and rafts to launch them. To the remainder of the convoy, creeping along in the darkness at ten knots, with no lights showing and trying to keep station, it was obvious what had happened. Quickly she fell out of line, letting the rest of the convoy go by. The explosion, the shouts and cries of the crew, the lights of hand torches, all told their story. The ship carried four lifeboats, but three days earlier, the convoy had run into a heavy gale with mountainous waves scattering the convoy over a wide area. In this storm, the davits of both port lifeboats had been badly damaged, making it impossible for the boats under them to be lowered. In the event, they were manually swung inboard and firmly lashed to the deck so that in the event of trouble they could be cut adrift and hopefully floated off as the ship sank. Unfortunately, the ship had also suffered other damage, which forced them to heave-to and drop out of the convoy in order to deal with the problems. Later, they caught up with the rest of the ships and regained their position as the leading ship in the twelfth column.

The commodore then signalled, 'Do you wish to return to

port to effect repairs?' To this, the captain replied that he
would have to consider the position and would advise him as
soon as possible as to his decision. By 2.30 that afternoon,
the commodore despatched another signal to the effect that
submarines were suspected of being in the area, and half an
hour later, an escorting destroyer came alongside the *Shillong*
asking the captain if he had yet reached a decision regarding
returning to port. The rest of his officers were unanimous in
advising the captain to return to New York, but he, on the
illogical premise that theirs was a 'lucky ship' and unlikely to
be torpedoed, considered it unnecessary. An absurd
superstition, which no doubt contributed to the later loss of
so many lives. This decision was then relayed to the
destroyer, which sped away to take up its appointed position
ahead of the convoy.

On this fateful night of the massive explosion, the *Shillong*
settled rapidly and within seven minutes, the main deck was
awash, with the propellers out of water, poised for the long,
deep plunge. In the wrecked bridge, the third officer and
Apprentice Browse seized a sextant and chronometer, but in
trying to make their way down the bridge ladder, a huge
wave swept inboard and carried the third officer away, not to
be seen again. In the meantime, the apprentice had reached
the deck with the water up to his waist, and, finding the rail,
dived overboard. Seconds later, as the cries of men in fear rose
above the wind, there came the suffocating stench of oil fuel
pouring out from the tanks.

A few moments before she went down, a crowd of men
could be seen herded together high in the stern, waving and
shouting as the ship hung there momentarily, before moving
slowly forward and downward. As the terror intensified,
some jumped feet first into the sea, and there struck out from
the ship as far as possible, panting and gasping from the
shock of the cold Atlantic water; others, too frightened to
jump, crawled further upward to the steepening lifting stern,
until at last, with the decision taken out of their hands, they
fell, tumbling over the stern with bloodcurdling screams, to
fall across the dripping propeller blades. The sea began to

spawn bobbing red lights of lifebelt bulbs, as men struck out to escape the suction of the sinking ship, and then, in pathetic little clusters, drifted together.

With the shrill hiss of escaping steam and the roar of tumbling machinery being torn from their bolted beds, *Shillong* took her final plunge, leaving a huge eddy of swirling bubbling water. For those in the sea, the smell of oil fuel was all too familiar. So often, far too often, in previous convoys they had smelt it when passing torpedoed ships. Now they were the victims. It had been twelve minutes from the time the torpedo struck.

Just before leaving the ship, Browse had spotted a raft some distance away, identified by hand torches from men who had climbed aboard it. With the high sea running, it was impossible to reach it by swimming, but fortunately a huge wave carried him in the opposite direction towards the only lifeboat that had been launched, and he was hauled aboard. It was later discovered that the second starboard lifeboat had capsized on becoming waterborne, resulting in the loss of the boat's wireless set which had been placed in it. This boat was much smaller,and, although successfully set down in the water, twenty or thirty native Lascars swarmed into it causing it to sink.

In the screaming confusion that followed, another apprentice Arthur Moore swam to a hatch board, floating nearby, and clung to it. Fifteen minutes later, his colleague Francis Parkins managed to join him, and there, in a violent storm-tossed sea they hung on to this, their only support. An hour and a half later, they sighted a raft crowded with men to whom they waved and shouted, and eventually the two units came near enough for the apprentices to swim over and join them. On this raft, there were twenty-two men including the captain, the chief and other officers, most of them engineers, two or three gunners and a number of natives. As there was no room on the raft, the two apprentices could only hang on to the sides.

Others were swimming around and around, struggling to reach the drifting raft, cursing and sobbing in the last stages of exhaustion. Some, thrashing about wildly, hysterically, having managed to reach the raft clung on to the looplines. Where there were no more places, they clung on to the men already there.

As the night wore on and the bitter cold robbed them of their strength, men began to die. A few died well, without fuss, silently, without a murmur, passing out of this life with quiet dignity. Others died badly, obstinately, complaining. Among these were the bitter, the selfish, the greedy, the pessimists, the grumblers and those for whom terror quickly brought the hand of death, dying protesting, cursing. As men died and drifted away, the empty places were quickly filled.

From midnight onward, the weather further deteriorated with a constant run of waves some forty or fifty feet high, lifting and tossing the raft around like a cork. Two hours later, it capsized several times, casting away most of those aboard it. Eventually it steadied, but by now only six remained. These were the captain, naval gunner Hadley, Third Engineer Macrae, Army gunner Thompson and the two apprentices Parkins and Moore. The captain was obviously dying and lay in the centre well of the raft, refusing to sit up, so that the waves were constantly washing over him. They made repeated attempts to lift him but in their weakened condition, found it difficult to move the eighteen-stone man.

By now, Parkins had begun to weaken. He lay prone on the raft and seemed to have no will to fight and later that morning he died, soon followed by the captain. The remaining four then managed to push the bodies overboard and settled down to await the coming of daylight. Fortunately, containers on the raft contained water and food and at that time there seemed reasonable prospects of survival. But as the grey streaks of dawn appeared and they found themselves looking out over a vast turbulent sea, with waves constantly trying to drag them off, hope gave place to despair.

However, during that morning, 5 April, as the raft rose and fell in the long, grey waves, they spotted the lifeboat a mile or so distant. By waving and shouting, they were able to attract attention, but the boat was unable to make any progress in the rough sea. In the event, the four on the raft managed to pick up some floating pieces of wood, and using these as paddles gradually moved towards the boat but this effort proved exhausting and it was not until four o'clock in the afternoon that they manoeuvred alongside. By this time, Macrae the engineer was in a bad way but they all managed to climb into the lifeboat.

The craft, badly overcrowded, now held thirty-eight men, twelve of these being British, the rest Lascars. As this was his station boat, fourth apprentice Coleman was in charge, but the cold and exposure of the previous night was beginning to take its toll, and it proved necessary to allow apprentice Browse, who had swum to the boat, to share command. The twelve British now comprised the three apprentices, Browse and Moore and Coleman, gunners Hadley, Barnes and Thompson, Engineer Macrae, radio operators Johnson and Benson and three seamen.

Towards evening, the wind increased with heavy seas breaking over the bow. To prevent capsizing, a sea anchor was put out with four men working the oars on the lee side to assist the anchor in keeping it head on to the waves. A new danger developed that evening as heavy floating hatch boards from the sunken ship were flung towards the boat threatening to stave in the sides. To combat this, Macrae, although in a bad way, quietly stationed himself in the bow with a boat hook and kept the debris away. He continued doing this until just before midnight, when he slid down into the bottom of the boat and died. The Lascars refused to do anything to help, so the watches were set among the British.

During that night, Apprentice Coleman died, so Browse as Senior Cadet took charge. The following morning, the senior radio operator lost his reason and became very violent, with some of the crew having to restrain him, but after two hours he calmed down, sank into a coma and quietly died. During the fourth day, Browse cut his hand badly when opening a tin of stores. It was thought at first that he had severed an artery and a tourniquet was applied but it proved not to be as bad as he had thought. After this, it seemed he could do very little, which imposed more work on the rest.

During the day, the sea anchor was carried away and they had to use anything they could find. The sails had been kept in reserve in the hope that if and when the wind changed to the west, they could be carried along eastward in the direction of Scotland not a thousand miles away. Browse insisted on using the sails as a sea anchor, despite the strong protests of the rest. Nevertheless, there was little else to use; all the bottom boards in the boat had been used and lost, and eventually he had his way. That sea anchor broke up during the night and by morning had been entirely carried away. As a last resort, two duffel coats over a grapnel with a couple of oars were lashed together to form some sort of drag which helped to keep the bows head on. As the Lascars refused to do anything to help, they were put into the bows, leaving them much to themselves.

The weather now turned extremely cold and limbs became numb and unresponsive, with everyone suffering from stomach cramp. At times, outer garments were frozen stiff with a film of ice over everything. In the high seas that were running, it was impossible to keep the boat dry and as a consequence their feet were in water all the time.

As a result, feet began to swell inside the sea-boots and it was found necessary to cut off the lower part of the boot, retaining only the upper for some sort of protection. Some of the men had no shoes at all, having kicked them off in the water when they abandoned ship. So intensive was the cold, that hands became fixed with cramp after each attempt at rowing, making it extremely difficult to unclasp them from the oars. By the fifth day, the wind had changed around to the west and, to aid their progress eastward, two blankets were sewn together and with the boat hook as mast, they rigged a sail of sorts and ran before the wind.

During the next few days, men died at intervals and their bodies dropped over the side and by 8 April, there were only ten left alive, one Lascar and nine British. It seemed now that it was only sheer determination and the will to live that kept the survivors going. On that afternoon, Radio Operator Benson who appeared to be in excellent physical condition and was only twenty-two, began to suffer from the cold and, giving up the fight to survive, quietly died.

The gunners Hadley and Barnes behaved magnificently during the entire ordeal. They were the only two men who remained cheerful and who did their utmost to keep up the spirits of the rest. They took advantage of the special oil in the store boxes, massaging their limbs and those of the others who were too exhausted. It was probably these vigorous movements which helped to maintain circulation and keep them alive. By the morning of 10 April, as dawn light lit the sky, it was found that the remaining native and two of the seamen had died during the night, which now left only six out of the original thirty-eight in the boat. Those not on watch sheltered in the after-well with blankets to protect them from the biting wind.

Morale at this time was at its lowest and it was difficult to persuade some to get up for their watches, but on the whole, they acted with courage, considering the severity of the ordeal which they were undergoing. At times, the nerves of some went to pieces and Apprentice Browse had to coax or bully them to pull themselves together. During the early days, the water ration had been limited to four ounces per man but as so many died, the ration was increased to six ounces.

Despite steady easterly progress aided by the tiny sail, it seemed impossible they could survive much longer. They estimated their position as approximately 900 miles west of Scotland and 600 miles south of Greenland, although in their weakened state this could well have been a miscalculation. To reach land before their strength failed was clearly out of the question, and although only one or two voiced that opinion, every man realized that survival now had to be measured not in terms of days but hours.

However, late in the morning of the twelfth day, as they sat or lay almost in a stupor, listening to the monotonous sound of the waves slapping against the boat and the moan and whistle of the wind raging over the top of the white-crested rollers, a new sound came to their ears, almost inaudible at first, just a faint hum growing in volume with the passing seconds. Barely able to stand, their brine-lidded eyes searched the restless ocean from horizon to horizon and found nothing, but the sound persisted. The adrenalin of hope had now set their pulses racing and, as though prompted by the same thought, they lifted their eyes skyward.

Against the racing clouds they saw it, a plane, just a speck at first but growing larger, heading eastward in their direction. A miracle, an answer to their secret anguished prayers. To a man they waved frantically, gabbling inarticulate cries for help from croaking throats. Then, as though fate had decided on one last cruel fling, the aircraft turned southwards. It must have been a mile away, and it would indeed have been a miracle of vision to have spotted such a small object as a lifeboat, no more than a grey dot against a grey ocean.

Cursing his slow-wittedness, Browse tore open the store locker and with trembling hands lit the two flares. Against the tumbling seas, the red flame and smoke showed up clearly, and seconds later, the plane turned towards them and was soon circling the boat. It proved to be a Catalina flying boat on patrol and, despite the fact that they had been seen and their plight acknowledged, the six survivors continued their frantic waving until utterly exhausted, then collapsed into the bottom of the boat, watching the aircraft circling.

Minutes later, the plane dropped a parcel wrapped in a life-jacket some way ahead of the boat, but such was their weakness they had no strength to lift an oar to row against the high seas, and had to simply watch the parcel float away. Five minutes later, the plane flew off but the fact that they had been seen and their position plotted, gave them every hope they would soon be picked up by a rescue ship. During the rest of the day, the weather again deteriorated and by late afternoon, sixty-foot high waves were running and several times the boat was on the verge of capsizing.

Early that evening, a Norwegian destroyer closed them.

The English-speaking captain was able to tell them that in these rough conditions it would be impossible to pick them up, as the boat would simply smash to pieces against the destroyer's side. They did however, make a lee by pumping oil on the water, but it had little effect. Two hours later, another ship arrived. This was the rescue vessel *Zamelek*. With the last remnants of their failing strength, they managed to pull the boat towards the vessel and by superb seamanship, the *Zamelek* put her bow alongside the lifeboat to make a good lee. Ladders and nets were placed over the side but the survivors were too weak to help themselves and as a consequence, large baskets were lowered, into which the men tumbled, and one by one were hauled up on deck.

Immediately they were taken to the sick bay and put to bed with electrically heated blankets, but as every man's feet were badly frost-bitten, these were kept outside the blankets on pillows. After five days in the rescue ship, thawing of the feet set in to give intense pain to the lucky ones. Those who felt no pain had to have feet or legs amputated. It was indeed a tragic end for the crew of the 'Lucky' *Shillong* whose luck had finally run out. Out of the total crew of seventy-eight, only six were pulled aboard the *Zamelek*.

10 The Convoy that Saved Malta

'Never in the field of human conflict was so much owed by so many to so few.'

These words, spoken by the Prime Minister, Winston Churchill in August 1940, were a tribute to the men of the Royal Air Force who saved Britain from defeat in the darkest days of World War II. Just two years later, those glowing terms of praise could equally have been paid to the men of the Merchant and Royal Navies, who fought the heroic convoy 'Pedestal' through to the harbour of Valetta in Malta.

Facing starvation and destruction, or ignominious capitulation, after months of daily German and Italian bombing, the arrival of the remnants of a battered and almost annihilated convoy raised new hopes and the will to survive. Pedestal has been established in history as the most ill-starred and bravest convoy that ever sailed to relieve Malta, with particular attention focused on the gallant oil tanker *Ohio*. The surrender of the island would have been a disaster of the first magnitude, resulting in an incalculable setback to Allied fortunes in the Mediterranean. Avoidance of such a catastrophe depended on the arrival of enough food to maintain the island's existence, and, militarily, adequate oil fuel to sustain warship and aircraft operations against the enemy supply route to its armies in Libya in North Africa.

The island of Malta has great strategic importance, in that

it sits astride the main shipping lanes between Gibraltar and the Suez Canal, and in World War II it provided a base to attack enemy supply convoys operating from Italy to their bases along the North African coast. These convoys supported the Axis troop's drive towards Alexandria in their bid to capture the Suez canal. It was Malta from which British submarines slid out to take their toll of the Axis convoys to Tripoli: Malta, that launched the Swordfish torpedo bombers and the Wellington heavy bombers to swoop on tankers and ammunition ships, whose cargoes were the very lifeblood of the offshore Italian Empire in North Africa; Malta, whose destroyers struck in the darkness and passed on, denying the enemy its power to build up supplies. But if Malta were eliminated, then there would be no stopping the German General, Field Marshal Irwin Rommel, Commander-in-Chief of the Italo-German forces in North Africa, in his advance eastward.

To the Maltese, eyes reddened with limestone dust and lack of sleep from the constant bombing, the German and Italian plan was simple enough. Based on overwhelming air superiority, operating from their airfields in Sicily, with practically unlimited replacements, the enemy aimed first of all at eliminating the island's airfields and fighter opposition; then it was to be the turn of the dockyard and submarine base, the shipping and essential services of the harbour; then would come the destruction of all stores, barracks and communications; and lastly, the mining of all approaches to the island so that no ships could come to the island's rescue. This programme, nicely rounded off, would have forced Malta to capitulate.

Although Malta was a tiny outpost, a mere dot in the vast area of that sea, it constituted a painful thorn in the sides of the two Axis powers, Germany and Italy. On the northern side of the Mediterranean, Hitler's troops occupied France, Yugoslavia, Greece, Bulgaria and Rumania. His partner Mussolini, boasted a navy of six modern battleships, thirty cruisers, sixty destroyers, seventy torpedo-boats and over one hundred submarines, and an air force of some 2,000 aircraft which could deploy from the Italian mainland or Sicily. And along the southern perimeter of the Mediterranean, Rommel's armies held the coastline from Tripolitania to Egypt. As for the British, despite the overwhelming odds, units of Admiral Sir Andrew Cunningham's meagre Eastern Mediterranean fleet, based at Alexandria, had inflicted heavy casualties on the Italian dictator's large but timorous navy. Nevertheless, Malta, so close to Sicily, was wholly vulnerable to constant bombing by the enemy air forces. When Italy entered the war in June 1940, the defences of the island were almost non-existent, except for a few anti-aircraft guns. There was no aircraft to constitute a fighter defence, no reserves of food, and if Italy had been on the ball they could have starved out the population in a matter of weeks.

As the number of supply ships from Italy and Greece in support of Rommel's forces increased, so did the importance of Malta's offensive operations, and though they could ill be spared from Britain's fragile air defences in 1941, Churchill insisted that the offensive operations should be sustained and given support to naval forays.

It was a timely intervention, for in the combined raids on the Axis heavily laden troop-ships, freighters and oil tankers, sailing from Italy, over seventy per cent were destroyed. With diminishing supplies, Rommel was forced to retreat and urgent appeals were made to Hitler to redress the situation by destroying Malta and thus remove the threat to his supply routes. Until now, Hitler had been preoccupied with his campaign against Russia, but, as the advance slowed in that enterprise, he began to realize the importance of supporting Rommel's drive to the east. As a result, thousands of aircraft were transferred to the Mediterranean and placed under the command of Field Marshall Kesselring as Commander-in-Chief (Air) South, who was given two tasks:

1 To achieve air and sea mastery in the area between Italy and North Africa and to suppress Malta.
2 To paralyse enemy traffic through the Mediterranean and stop supplies reaching Malta.

The violence and fury of those attacks on Malta was crushing. Hardly a single day or night passed without bombing raids. During 1942, the attacks sometimes totalled over three hundred per month or, on an average, every two and a half hours. Although desperate resistance was put up by the defence aircraft, the harbour was left in ruins; over 30,000 houses destroyed or heavily damaged and one hundred churches gutted. In one month alone, 6,000 tons of high explosives fell upon towns and villages, resulting in over 1,300 being killed and 1,600 seriously wounded. The scale of the attacks not only reduced the island's offensive capability but made it hard put even to defend itself.

Even worse, with Kesselring's control of the air over the western and eastern Mediterranean, it paralysed British convoy supplies trying to reach the island. By August 1942, the brave defenders, though fighting back, realized that unless food and oil reached the island within three weeks, the population of 250,000 would reach starvation and finally capitulation.

In May 1942, Churchill pressed the Commander-in-Chief of the British Desert Forces in the Middle East, Field Marshall Sir Claude Auchinleck to launch an offensive to relieve Malta. In his letter to Auchinleck on 8 May he said:

> The loss of Malta would be a disaster of the first magnitude to the British Empire and probably fatal in the long run to the defence of the Nile. We are determined that Malta shall not be allowed to fall without a battle being fought by your whole army for its retention. The starving out of this fortress would involve the surrender of over 300,000 men, army and air force, together with several hundred guns. Its possession would give the enemy a clear and sure bridge to Africa, with all the consequences flowing from that.

Churchill left no doubt in Auchinleck's mind on how the British War Cabinet felt about the importance of Malta.

The two main commodities for Malta's existence were flour and fuel oil, the latter being a requisite for heating, lighting and cooking. Electric power for hospitals, bakeries, factories, water-supply and sewage works all depended on oil. Even if one or two ships did reach the island, Malta's own oil-driven minesweepers had to clear the channel and the Grand Harbour approaches of mines which had been dropped the night before by enemy aircraft and submarines. More important though, oil and aviation spirit were vital to maintain defensive and offensive operations. If the planes could not fly, then Malta would be impotent, utterly at the mercy of the enemy. It can therefore be seen that although flour was highly important, oil became the substance upon which the fate of the island depended.

The enemy's massive air deployment covering some 3,000 square miles around Malta ensured that few surface ships ever reached the garrison. And time was running out for the defenders. By the beginning of August, despite severe rationing, the population had barely three weeks supplies left and the defending aircraft barely enough aviation spirit to fly their planes. In the minds of the British War Cabinet in London one thought remained uppermost; Malta had to be supplied, whatever the cost. A few weeks earlier, Lieutenant-General Sir W. Dobbie, Governor of Malta, had asked to be relieved from his post. The long strain of responsibility of trying to provide dwindling rations to a quarter of a million civilians and thousands of troops, with little hope of remedy, and under constant bombing, had taken its toll. With the greatest regret, Churchill had to accept the resignation and to appoint a successor. The choice fell on Field Marshal Viscount Gort, the Governor of Gibraltar, whom Churchill considered as a warrior of the truest mettle. Early in May, General Dobbie had submitted to the War Office an assessment of the island's supply position. It was grave indeed. When Lord Gort arrived and made his own valuation with the Chiefs of the Navy, Army and Air Force, he found that Dobbie's report in no way exaggerated the seriousness of the position.

The stark realization of the situation left him with no alternative but to submit to Whitehall a date upon which capitulation would be inevitable. Unless sufficient supplies arrived in time, 'Surrender date' would have to be no later than the first week of September. Any delay in surrender, would mean extensive deaths from starvation among the population. He was careful to point out to the Prime Minister that 'it is purely a question of survival'. The general overall situation of the Middle East was deteriorating anyway, and by Kesselring's neutralization of the island, Axis supplies into Libya rapidly increased, and Rommel, now able to renew his assault, drove the British Army back to within a few miles of Alexandria. At the War Cabinet Defence Committee meeting. at the end of April, which was headed by Churchill as Minister of Defence, and included the former Prime Minister Neville Chamberlain, the gravity of the situation was expressed in no uncertain terms and drastic measures were called for.

To send a number of cargo ships through the Mediterranean at the normal convoy speed of seven knots would be suicidal. Freighters of at least sixteen knots would be necessary, but while these could be supplied, no British oil tankers existed which would reach that speed, and oil was the vital factor. As a result of diplomatic negotiations and the generous attitude of the United States, the Defence Committee were informed that two of America's finest and fastest oil tankers belonging to the Texas Oil company would be made available.

While the Admiralty had little doubt of the necessity of fighting a convoy through, they were fully aware of the cost in lives and ships that might have to be made. The outline plan which they were directed to implement, was to escort fourteen heavily laden merchant ships, including the fast American oil tanker *Ohio* through the Mediterranean from Gibraltar to Malta, under the code name 'Pedestal'. The War Cabinet, irrespective of the risk involved and ready to accept the danger of great losses, were determined to prosecute the convoy's drive eastward with all vigour.

The approximate distance from Gibraltar to the island was some 1,100 miles and while the first two thirds of the voyage would be perilous and subject to heavy attack, the most critical and dangerous stretch would be the Narrows. This channel, lying between the south-western coast of Sicily and the Cape Bon peninsular on the north African shore, constituted the gravest problem in the planning, a veritable gauntlet between two enemy held territories. To accompany the fourteen merchant ships in stages through to Malta would be a massive escort fleet of fifty British warships including battleships, aircraft-carriers, cruisers and destroyers.

'Pedestal' was to be a high-speed convoy to minimize losses, but due to Britain's mercantile sinkings in the Atlantic, these vessels were difficult to locate. Eventually, thirteen large cargo ships with attainable speeds of sixteen knots were found, and these, detached from their current assignments, were at once hurried to the ports of the Clyde, Liverpool and Bristol for loading. With inevitable losses in mind, each ship was allocated a mixture of supplies, the bulk of which was flour but also a percentage of petrol and aviation spirit in five-gallon cans, and ammunition; the last two, a lethal combination for an expedition with such sinister prospects.

Two vital commodities, kerosene and fuel oil would have to be carried in bulk, and for this, a special tanker would be needed. Therefore, the American tanker *Ohio*, the only suitable vessel to meet the requirements of speed and size was called upon to join the convoy in an effort to break the blockade. How vital she became in this historic convoy will be seen by the efforts of the enemy to destroy her and of the British to save her. *Ohio*, long remembered by the public, was to become the most famous of all the Mediterranean merchant ships, and by her success became the greatest single contribution towards Malta's survival. Launched in 1940, by the Sun Shipbuilding Company in Chester, Pennsylvania, she was taken over by the Texas Oil Company, now Texaco. By an arrangement between the British and American governments, she arrived in the Clyde in June and was at once requisitioned for special duty.

Instructed by the Ministry of War Transport, the British Eagle Oil and Shipping Company assumed temporary

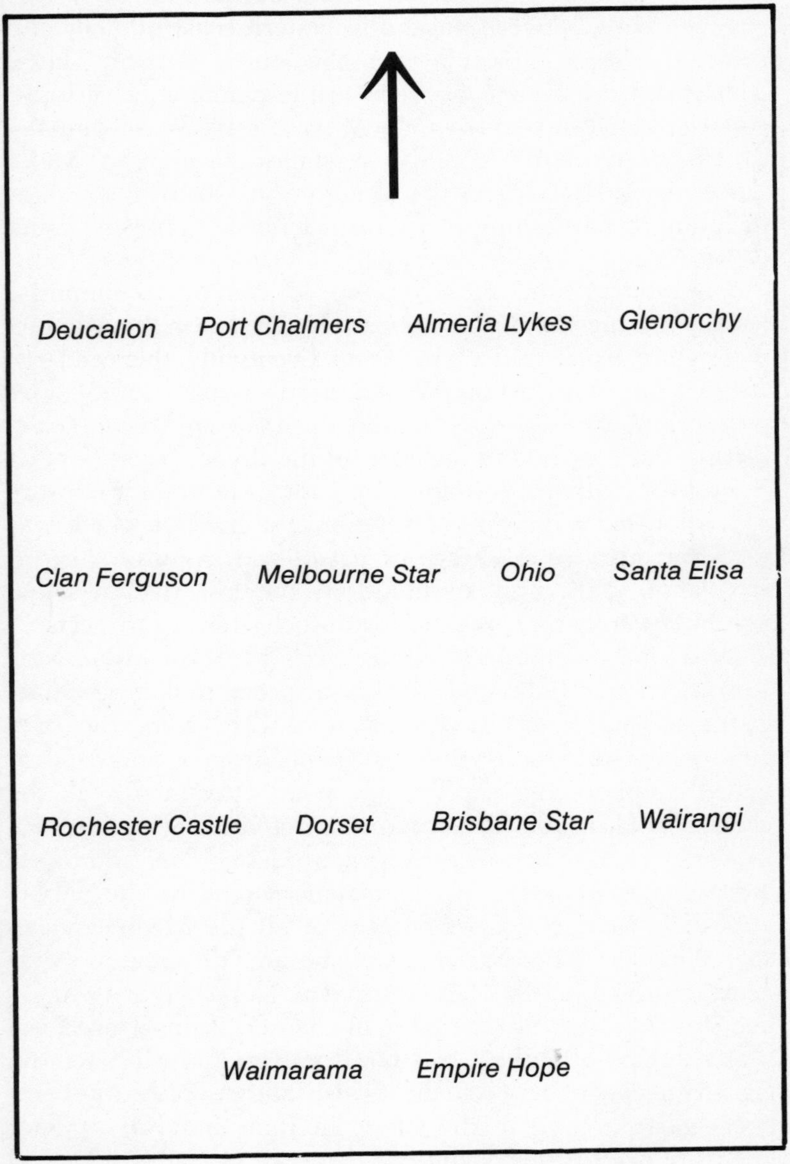

Deucalion   Port Chalmers   Almeria Lykes   Glenorchy

Clan Ferguson   Melbourne Star   Ohio   Santa Elisa

Rochester Castle   Dorset   Brisbane Star   Wairangi

Waimarama   Empire Hope

Fig. 3   Pedestal Convoy for Malta.
Disposition of cargo ships – 10–11 August 1942

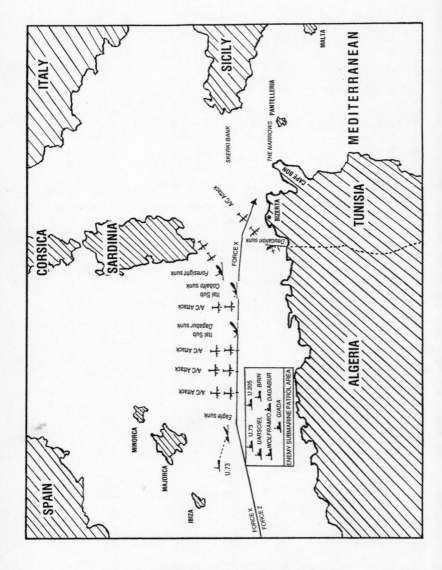

Fig. 4   Result of enemy action 11–12 August 1942.

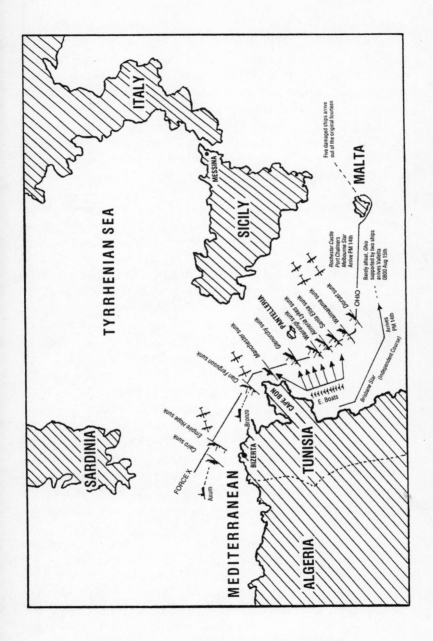

Fig. 5   Result of enemy action 12–13 August 1942.

ownership. The United States at that time was not in the war and in accordance with International Law, its American crew were not involved. Innocent of the reason, and much to their displeasure, they were disembarked and replaced with a British crew under the command of one of the Company's youngest masters, Captain Dudley W. Mason, aged thirty-nine. To avoid damage from shock explosions, modifications were carried out on the engine mountings and the installation of ten light guns. Naval gunners were brought aboard to augment the crew, to bring its complement to seventy-seven.

These alterations completed, on 28 July, she moved down the Clyde to pump her cargo aboard — 8,900 tons of fuel oil, 2,000 tons of kerosene, and 2,000 tons of diesel oil, a total of 12,900 tons.

Thus, the 'Pedestal' convoy of fourteen freighters with their precious merchandise totalling 85,000 tons was made up of the following ships: *Empire Hope, Wairangi, Waimarama, Glenorchy, Santa Elisa, Dorset, Brisbane Star, Melbourne Star, Clan Ferguson, Rochester Castle, Almeria Lykes, Deucalion, Port Chalmers* and *Ohio.*

While all these complicated arrangements for the mission were being put in hand, Italian and German forces, from leaked information, were able to take the necessary measures, right to the last detail, to prepare their plans to destroy 'Pedestal'. The freighters from Liverpool and Bristol, arrived at Gourock on the morning of 2 August to join the remainder of the convoy. During the day, Rear-Admiral Burrough summoned aboard his flagship *Nigeria* all the masters of the merchant ships and explained the plans of the operation in great detail.

At 6 p.m., the ships got under way and, led by the commodore's vessel *Port Chalmers*, made their passage through the Clyde in single line ahead, out into open water. It was one of those evenings when the Scottish Highlands were at their best and many of the crews, who watched the gold- and red-streaked sky descending over the islands of Bute and Arran, must have wondered if they would ever return to see them again. Sadly, many were to perish in this endeavour to bring relief to the starving island of Malta.

On Monday 10 August, the fourteen merchant ships with their massive escort of fifty warships passed through the straits of Gibraltar and into the Mediterranean. German and Italian Intelligence were not only aware of the presence of the convoy but also of its purpose. As a result, every available aircraft under the command of Field Marshal Kesselring, with his headquarters in southern Italy, was made ready with orders to attack and destroy every ship. Not a single vessel must be allowed to reach the island – that was the order.

Several accounts have been written of the frightening losses sustained by the Royal Naval warships during the next five days and nights in their endeavour to protect the fourteen merchant ships against the overwhelming and massive efforts of the enemy. Five days and nights of non-stop battles against enemy submarines, torpedo-boats and thousands of bomber aircraft, in which the Royal Navy suffered the grievous loss of one aircraft-carrier, two cruisers and one destroyer sunk, in addition to one aircraft-carrier, two cruisers and one destroyer badly damaged, and also, of more importance, the loss of many fine men.

While these accounts have given full prominence to this facet of the Malta epic, little has been recorded of the magnificent and heroic actions in which the Merchant Navy was involved and the sacrifices made to bring their life-saving cargoes to the island of Malta. Although Royal Naval warships received the impact of the enemy's wrath because of their gallant anti-aircraft retaliation, the main target for the German and Italian bombers was the struggling freighters. During those five days and nights, thousands of bombs were dropped around and on the fourteen merchant vessels of which only five survived to reach the island. The experiences of some of these fine ships are herewith recorded.

'Pedestal' was the most important and impressive convoy of the Mediterranean war, in which this massive fleet of warships, made up of aircraft-carriers, battleships, cruisers and destroyers formed a protective screen around the little fleet of merchant vessels. The importance of these freighters cannot be over-emphasized, for it was upon their safe arrival that the survival of Malta depended.

The first of the enemy attacks began that same afternoon, resulting in the torpedoeing of the aircraft-carrier *Eagle* with the loss of 130 men. For the next two days, the convoy was subjected to mass attacks by hundreds of high-level, dive and torpedo bombers. In each attack, amidst an indescribable din of anti-aircraft fire from warships and merchant ships alike and the smell of burning cordite, the sky above the convoy was filled with bursting shells and whining bullets.

Despite this, some of the planes came on, diving from different points, picking their targets. From each plane the bombs hurtled down, falling over and over, just missing freighters and warships, exploding on impact with the sea. Huge pillars of water, boiling up from underwater explosions, cascaded over gun crews, submerging them in their gun pits and open positions. Numbed and gasping from the deluge, they scrambled back, fingers clutching for triggers.

Temporarily repulsed by the withering gunfire of the defences, the Junker dive-bombers concentrated on the freighter *Deucalion*, a Blue Funnel line ship, a veteran of the Malta run. The lead ship in the port column, she carried a large number of passengers for Malta, which with the naval and army gunners, totalled 122.

As the aircraft screamed down almost vertically from 3,000 feet, the gunners went into action, pumping shells into the power-diving planes. Two were clawed out of the sky, the starboard wing of one torn away, to cartwheel into the sea on the starboard quarter; the other, with black smoke pouring from its fuselage and its engines roaring to a deafening crescendo, nose-dived into the water to disintegrate into a mass of flame and smoke. Despite this success, *Deucalion* was doomed, for seconds later she was straddled by five 500-lb bombs. Four of these were very near misses, lifting the 7,500-ton ship almost out of the water but the fifth was dead on target. It plunged through the deck, penetrated no. 5 hold and broke out through the side of the ship to explode in a blinding flash. *Deucalion* slowed to a standstill, and her master, Captain R. Brown, made a quick assessment of the damage. Two holds were filled with water to deck level and cargo was falling out from the hole in the ship's side.

Yet the vessel was still afloat, and as her engines were undamaged, Brown decided to proceed at a much reduced speed in the hope of saving his ship and the valuable cargo. As the rest of the convoy caught up and passed the damaged ship, they soon left her far behind, alone on the western horizon. The crews of the distancing ships must have wondered, if in the hours to come, that too might be their fate. Unknown to Captain Brown, a number of the crew had panicked and taken to the boats. These were made up of greasers and stewards who had swung out two lifeboats. It was no reflection on the normal Blue Funnel Line crew, for most of the complement had been taken from the Merchant Navy pool of labour, before sailing, and were apparently reluctant to accept the self-discipline normally associated with company men.

It was a most unfortunate episode, for almost an hour was wasted in getting them and the boats back on board, while the ship itself became a sitting duck for skulking submarines. The engines were restarted and at a crawling pace of seven knots *Deucalion* set off again. At this time, the destroyer *Bramham* was detached from the warship escort and sent back to accompany the stricken ship.

It was impossible for the freighter to catch up with the convoy, so with the destroyer they tried to use the inshore passage close to the Tunisian coast. Now southward bound and listing, *Deucalion* followed *Bramham* for the tricky passage towards the infamous area known as the Narrows. This channel lies between the south-western coast of Sicily and the Cape Bon peninsular on the north African shore. At the western end lies the Skerki Bank, an area of shallow water and at the eastern end the formidable fortress of Pantelleria, occupied then by the Italians. By taking this course, they hoped that they could sneak through and reach the beleaguered island.

This, however, was not to be, for their course was observed and reported to the Luftwaffe, who that evening found them again. In the dusk of the summer night, two dive-bombers roared in over the coastline and dropped three bombs, all just missing, and had it not been for her sturdy construction, the resultant explosions against the hull plates must surely have sunk her, but she remained afloat. Again hopes were raised, but not for long, for thirty minutes later, two Heinkel torpedo-bombers found her. They came in low, quietly, perhaps they had cut their engines until the last moment.

Almost too late, the guns of *Deucalion* went into action setting up a wall of flak which might have deterred most pilots. Almost contemptuously, they came on, pressing home their attack with suicidal courage, weaving a path through the shell-fire. The experts at home, with their mass of statistics, would have us believe that there is no target so easy to hit as a torpedo-plane approaching head-on. In practice, it never works that way. Throughout the war, in the Mediterranean, the Arctic and the Pacific, the immunity of the torpedo-bombers in the number of successful attacks carried out in the face of saturation defensive fire, constantly confounded the intellectual strategists. And this was no exception. The two planes came in together, almost wing-tip to wing-tip, bravely steadying on their target, despite being rocked by shrapnel. In a desperate bid to save his ship, Brown tried to turn *Deucalion* parallel to the course of the torpedoes. But it was too late and with little way on the vessel, the attempt failed. The plane to the left dropped its torpedo less than 400 yards away, pulled up in a maximum climb to port, just clearing the deck and disappeared into the gloom.

The second plane's pilot resolutely held on, and when only three hundred yards distant and barely fifty feet above the surface, he pressed the firing tit. With engines roaring at full power and banking steeply to the right, he just managed to clear the bows, with the tip of the starboard wing kissing the sea. The torpedo struck the water dead on course, running shallow, indeed it was impossible to miss. At forty-five miles an hour, it would take less than fifteen seconds to cover the distance. And that's all the time the gunners and watchers on *Deucalion* had.

Fifteen seconds of realization, knowing that the torpedo was homing in on the ship's hull knowing exactly where, inside the steel plating, lay hundreds of cans of kerosene and highly volatile aviation spirit, so dangerous it could even be ignited from the spark of a careless boot. It seemed that death was but a flicker of an eyelid away. And yet, by an incomprehensible twist of fortune, it was the blast that saved them. The initial shock wave from the explosions, blasting upwards, rupturing the deck, blew them away from the sheet of flame that followed and grew into a billowing pillar of fire that lit the evening sky for miles. Those nearest the seat of the explosion were sent hurtling across the deck, arms flaying the air. Miraculously, only one man was killed, Gunner Hutchinson. The rest, though suffering from broken arms and legs, lacerations and bruises, survived.

Gunner Mead, badly wounded, caught under a pile of flying debris, was trapped beneath a liferaft. The ship threatened to blow up at any moment, for the bulkheads at the seat of the fire were becoming red-hot, with the imminent certainty of igniting the high octane fuel in the adjacent hold. Despite this, two midshipmen struggled to free him and, having done so, supported him in the water until the destroyer picked them up. Those who failed to reach the one or two lifeboats available saved their lives by jumping into the sea where they were recovered by the circling *Bramham*.

The freighter was now ablaze from end to end but still afloat, and to hasten her end, the commanding officer of *Bramham*, Lieutenant Baines, catapulted a depth-charge from the destroyer on to the deck of the sinking ship. This failed to explode, but as her end was obviously near he steamed away. Minutes later, in one enormous explosion, *Deucalion* blew up. After an extensive search for further survivors, *Bramham* set course to join the convoy with an additional 120 persons aboard.

In the fading light of the third day, 'Pedestal' entered the narrow navigable channel off the Tunisian coast, and the convoy formed into a long double line in order to thread its way through the hazardous waters. Following the convoy was the Italian submarine *Axum*, commanded by Lieutenant Ferrini. Rising to periscope depth, he saw two cruisers and a large oil tanker. Turning towards the target he fired all four bow torpedoes in spread formation. The first struck the cruiser *Nigeria*, the second and third, the cruiser *Cairo* and the fourth the tanker *Ohio*. This brilliant but possibly lucky salvo brought about a triple disaster of the worst order. In the gathering dusk, the whole force was thrown into confusion. The blaring of sirens and the fluttering of half-seen signals compounded the disorder. Destroyers raced in all directions at full speed, torn between the urgency of assisting the stricken ships and the necessity of destroying the enemy before more ships were hit. *Nigeria* was so badly damaged she had to return to Gibraltar, but *Cairo* was doomed and after some time she sank deeper and deeper until disappearing beneath the waters.

The third torpedoed ship, the oil tanker *Ohio* was also in trouble. At almost the same moment that *Cairo* just ahead was hit, a torpedo slammed into her port side. The explosion hurled many of the crew across the decks, as a bright flash lit up the sky and a great column of water reached above mast height. A second later, a pillar of flame roaring in its intensity shot high into the sky. The 9,000-ton tanker, her steering badly damaged, slewed around crazily, turning in circles. Her master, Captain Dudley Mason, rang 'Stop engines', while overhead, the dive-bombers screamed down bracketing the ship. Immediately astern was the 13,000-ton freighter *Empire Hope*, whose master, Captain G. Williams, was confronted with what seemed an inevitable collision with a burning tanker.

In a brilliantly executed manoeuvre, with engines revving at full speed astern, *Empire Hope* swung to port and sheered past *Ohio* less than a hundred feet away, aware only of a confused picture of roaring columns of flame and smoke. To Captain Mason, it seemed that his ship was finished. The deck on the port side had been ripped up and laid back inboard almost to centre line like the lid of a sardine can, bringing down a large derrick. The flying bridge was also destroyed and the pump room at the seat of the explosion was a shambles. Here, the ship's side had been opened up to form a hole some thirty feet by twenty-five feet, rupturing the kerosene and gas-oil tanks, the flaming contents of which were now pouring out freely into the sea.

With flames roaring up through some of the hatches, Mason gave the order for the engine-room to be cleared and the men brought up from below. He was left with the options of abandoning ship or fighting the fires with the risk of the crew being blown up. He decided to fight the fires, for, although every cargo was vital for the survival of Malta, oil was probably the most important. In a rallying appeal to his crew, a concerted attack on the flames was launched and later, with the assistance of the sea pouring through the torn side, they managed to extinguish all the fires. It was not made any easier by the constant bombing attacks concentrated on them, and the ship shuddered under the impact of several near misses. With the fires under control, the engines were successfully started and the emergency steering gear aft made ready. Although steering was difficult, the damaged tanker set off.

Meanwhile, after the near collision, *Empire Hope* had also received attention from the bombers. Despite Captain Williams' clever weaving through twenty near misses, and his gunners standing at their posts to fight off the constant attacks, *Empire Hope* was bracketed by a volley of bombs which brought her to a standstill with a large hole in her side. Now stationary, she soon received two direct hits. The first, exploding in no. 4 hold, where ammunition and oil was stored, erupted upwards, blowing away the 200 tons of coal stowed on top of the hatch. This succeeded in destroying many of the lifeboats and filling half the remainder with coal. Gouts of fire from the effect of the second bomb quickly spread to reach the area where high octane spirit was stored. This ignited instantly and was soon pouring over the hull to set the surrounding sea afire in a carpet of flame. With the after part of the ship a blazing inferno, the water-pumps smashed and the wheel jammed, causing it to turn in a wide circle, there was no alternative but to abandon the vessel. This was carried out so hurriedly, with the imminent possibility of the ammunition blowing up, that Captain Williams and the chief engineer were left on board. One of the boats returned to the ship. While waiting for it, Chief Engineer Henry Leffler calmly changed into his best uniform.

No praise is too high for the courage and fortitude of the gunners of *Empire Hope*, a tribute which could also be paid to all those on the merchant ships who stood by their guns under such fearsome attacks. Every gun position on the freighters was exposed; lacking frontal protection; these gunners had no illusions as to their life expectancy in the Mediterranean battles. It was these men who were exposed to the savage raking of machine-gun fire of low flying Junkers and bore the brunt of the flesh-tearing shrapnel of bombs that hit the decks to explode on impact. This was tragically evidenced on *Empire Hope* when several of her gunners, terribly injured, were blown overboard by the force of the blasts. Just after 9 p.m. that evening, the destroyer *Penn*, under Lieutenant-Commander J. Swain, appeared and picked up the survivors from the sea. She fired a torpedo to sink the blazing wreck, which, sizzling and spluttering in strident protest, vanished beneath a sea of flame.

As an award for the manner in which he had so brilliantly handled his ship in this blitzkrieg action, Captain Williams was awarded the DSC, an oustanding award usually only ascribed to the Royal Navy.

During this action, the large 13,000-ton freighter *Brisbane Star* was torpedoed. The explosion tore a huge hole in her bows, destroying the forward bulkheads. The water pouring in brought her to a standstill, and under such enormous pressure there was the imminent danger that other bulkheads would give way and flood the ship. Under the calm direction of her master, Captain R. Riley, the bulkheads were not only shored up and other damage repaired but the ship got under way again, albeit at only five knots. He decided that he was now so far behind the convoy, that the best chance of survival would be to hug the Tunisian coast and try to reach Malta as opportunity offered. With a prayer that this risky venture would be successful, Riley swung the helm to starboard and, under the groaning protests of the buckled plates, she limped away into the darkness. Against all odds and by fine seamanship, he reached Valetta some days later with the majority of his ship's desperately needed cargo intact.

At about the same time that *Empire Hope* was torpedoed, a Heinkel torpedo-bomber scored a direct hit on the *Clan Ferguson* under Captain A.H. Cossar. This vessel carried a lethal combination cargo of 7,000 tons, including 2,000 tons of aviation spirit and 1,500 tons of high explosives. The effect of the torpedo impact on the ship was instant. It triggered off a massive explosion. One moment she was weaving her way through the bomb splashes in the darkening gloom, the next she was literally blown apart. The eruption sent a pillar of flame and smoke hundreds of feet high. The two nearest ships, the *Wairangi* and *Glenorchy*, took the full force of the blast, as the searing heat and the waft of burning oil and paint and cordite enveloped them.

Many lethal things whistled through the air that night: chunks of the ship, bits and pieces of jagged steel plating, hatch covers, sections of bridge structure and remnants of steel ammunition boxes rained down upon the passing ships. What was to be seen of *Clan Ferguson* was merely the remnants of the upper deck and the upper hull, floating uncertainly within a sea of burning debris and flaming oil. Ripped open from stem to stern, dragged down by sheer weight of metal, she settled deeper and deeper and then disappeared. It seemed impossible that anyone could have escaped the holocaust, and yet out of the crew and passengers of some 125 persons, 60 survived. Those who were blown into the sea managed to cling to and climb aboard rafts that had broken loose. But their situation became desperate when they found themselves surrounded by a sea of fire, constantly kindled by rising fuel oil and by cans of aviation spirit floating to the surface, bursting and igniting.

An outstanding act of heroism was performed when eighteen-year-old cadet Allson paddled around among the blazing oil on a small raft, collecting survivors and placing them on a larger raft. He was responsible for saving eighteen men in this manner; his bravery was later recognized by the award of medals. For many hours flames licked the oil-covered surface, with black smoke rising like a funeral pyre drifting over the sea, marking the grave of *Clan Ferguson*. As the rafts gradually drew away from the burning sea, the men clinging to them assumed they were the only survivors, but dawn on the 13th revealed that other rafts were drifting not far distant.

During that day, an Italian submarine later identified as the *Bonzo* surfaced nearby, and the survivors were questioned by its captain concerning their ship. In the afternoon, a German Dornier flying boat from Sicily landed on the sea and picked up a number of men from the rafts, including those badly burned, and during the evening, a small Italian Red Cross seaplane picked up as many men as it could carry and took off. At about this time, an Italian E-boat took Captain Cossar and several men off his raft, when about a mile off the Tunisian coast, and flew them to Italy.

Admiral Burrough was rightly concerned about the losses the convoy had suffered. Six ships had gone in two days, and they still had nearly 300 miles to go before they reached the shelter of land.

Among the remaining merchant ships plodding steadily on, exhaustion was already taking its toll among the crews. They had been at action stations for almost forty hours without sleep, ready for instant activity, carrying out 1001 duties brought about by enemy action. Behind them lay peace unknown and rest impossible, rushed meals of cocoa and sandwiches. There was no safety below decks; there it was worse, for always there was the fear of being trapped in a sinking ship. Of all sounds on this earth there is none more likely to stamp itself upon a man's memory than the shrill, harsh klaxon call of 'Emergency action stations'. It is a pitched whistle, flailing the eardrums, alternating, pulsating with desperate urgency and impending danger. It brings a man, no matter how weary, no matter how exhausted, to his feet in seconds, with the heart beating like a hammer as he prepares to meet the unknown emergency. And there was always the never-to-be-forgotten clanging of boots on steel as men rushed up or down ladders to reach their posts, echoing to the sounds of cursing, running, half-dressed men. They had to preserve alertness and keyed-up efficiency, difficult things to maintain even in normal circumstances.

As the ships steamed past the northern edge of Cape Bon, it seemed very quiet, in fact too quiet. The only sounds to be heard were the hum of the ventilation shafts, the dull throb of engines and the gurgle of water streaming off the bows. As the ominous seconds ticked past the hour of midnight it heralded another period of nerve-racking tension. Waiting in the shadows of the Tunisian coast and unknown to the convoy, were twenty Italian motor torpedo boats.

Just after 2 a.m., the 9,000-ton freighter *Glenorchy* was suddenly illuminated in the glaring searchlight of one of these boats, which roared towards her on the port side and fired two torpedoes, both on target. Immediately, the ship listed to port with the sea pouring into the engine-room. With her cargo of aviation spirit and in the certainty she would blow up, several of the crew threw rafts overboard, and following the master, Captain Leslie's order to abandon ship, jumped in after them. Tom Brunskill, second engineer was in the engine-room when the torpedo entered and exploded. It killed the chief engineer, another second engineer, two junior engineers and two greasers. His report states:

> I myself was trapped underneath a grating and there was 45 feet of water mixed with oil above me. I was wearing a life-jacket at the time which kept me trapped beneath the grating but there is a limited time you can live under those conditions. I had made up my mind that my time had come and remember making my peace with God.
>
> All I remember is that by dint of struggling I came up and was able to breathe fresh air but unfortunately I was blinded by the oil. I felt my way along to where I knew the exit was

and grasped the rail that would lead me to the deck. My eyes were starting to see again, and when I arrived on deck a boat was being lowered but I did not have the strength to climb over the rail into it. Someone came behind me, grabbed me by the heels and pitched me over the side, where I hit the bottom of the boat and promptly passed out. Once the Third Mate had checked that everyone alive had cleared the vessel, Captain Leslie ordered the boats to go, but he himself refused to leave, despite constant appeals from his officers and men.

The boats finally reached the Tunisian coast where the majority were interned by the Vichy French. The following morning, the Mate, Mr Simon, with a number of volunteers went back to the still floating *Glenorchy* to once again try to persuade the Captain to leave. However, as they approached the ship, it capsized and sank following a heavy explosion which set fire to the oil on the water. Captain Leslie was not seen again but he obviously had very special personal reasons for sacrificing his life.

The Review magazine
Naval Historical Collectors & Research Association

Just after 3 a.m., another E-boat attack developed and, although strafed by a barrage of shellfire, the leading boats launched torpedoes which hit the freighter *Wairangi*. The resultant explosions produced a list to port and heavy flooding. With the ship still afloat however, the gunners fought on, strafing other E-boats. Remarkably, the impact of the torpedo produced little smoke, no spectacular explosion. But ripped open deep under the water-line she settled deeper and deeper, and it was only the strength of her bulkheads and the amount of trapped air which kept her afloat. Every effort was made to restart the engines but all to no avail. With no hope of salvaging the vessel, Captain Gordon decided to scuttle her. Charges were set and, after standing off in the boats and following the explosion, it was seen that *Wairangi* was sinking too slowly. A volunteer crew returned to the ship to hasten her end, but she was still afloat by dawn of the following day and had to be left, although her sinking was inevitable with her stern awash and the list to port much increased.

The E-boats were having a field-day, a regular 'Turkey shoot'. The next to go was the *Almeria Lykes*. When the attack came at about 3.15 a.m., the crew had little warning. The enemy, racing out of the darkness amid lethal machine-gun fire and exploding shells, fired a torpedo which, ploughing into the port side of no. 1 hold, sent the 8,000-ton freighter over on to her starboard side, scattering men and equipment in all directions. She fell back to port with a heavy list, still floating but mortally wounded. Such had been the force of the explosion that the ship was split across the deck right to the keel with the forward bulkhead torn apart.

Almeria Lykes, like a wounded bird from a flight of geese falling out of line, drifted to a stop, to lie motionless. Reluctant to die, still afloat and rolling gently, she, like the not too distant *Glenorchy* and *Wairangi*, became silhouetted in the glow of the flickering burning surface oil against the black shadow of the sea. Fortunately, most of the crew escaped in boats but with the ship refusing to sink and aware of the danger that she might fall into enemy hands, the captain and several officers returned aboard to set scuttling charges. These exploded successfully, but seemed to make little difference and there she remained.

So far, the 8,000-ton *Santa Elisa* had borne a charmed life. Near-missed by dive-bombers, torpedo-bombers and E-boats, she had, by clever manipulation of the helm, survived as one of the last seven merchant ships. This distinction was soon terminated, when, after beating off an attacking E-boat which zoomed in on the port side, firing its machine-guns and killing several of the ship's gunners, another E-boat roared in on the opposite side to fire a torpedo at point-blank range. Once again, aviation spirit became the critical factor, for hundreds of cans of this lethal cargo ignited in a massive explosion. The blaze went out of control and engulfed the whole ship, forcing men to leap over the side regardless of whether they could swim or not. Three boats launched from aft managed to get away, but they were barely clear of the ship when the *Santa Elisa* blew up in a blinding flash which lit the sky for miles.

As the destroyer *Penn* moved in to pick up survivors, every detail of the burning decks could be seen; the roaring flames illuminating the three boats which crept towards them, accompanied by faint shouting, bobbing lights from lifebelted men in the water and pleas for help from struggling swimmers. Almost half the crew had been killed, including those who had little chance of escaping from the engine- and boiler-rooms. Admiral Burrough's trailing charges had now been reduced to six. Six out of the fourteen that had set sail from Gibraltar only three days ago. But to him and all the men of 'Pedestal', it must have seemed like a lifetime. At this time there had been no news of *Brisbane Star*.

The Burning Sea

Early on the morning of the 13th, with the convoy's crew still at action stations from the night's battles with E-boats, the lightening skies brought the dreaded sound of enemy aircraft. The pulsating throb of engines was a sound all too familiar, growing louder and louder every second; Junker 88s, flying in perfect formation, were escorted by squadrons of fighter planes, big twin-engined bombers each with a four-man crew crammed tightly in the nose, their deadly pay-loads, four 550-lb bombs carried externally under the wings.

Peeling off in twos and threes, they came hurtling down from 3,000 feet, several targeting the *Waimarama* carrying a deck cargo of several hundred cans of petrol. From the moment the Junkers began their dives, travelling at over 400 miles per hour, the men manning the ship's guns had less than six seconds to swing on to their targets in an attempt to destroy the diving aircraft. There were barely two seconds in which they could claim direct targeting. Any man who has experienced that moment and survived will carry the searing memory of it to the end of his days: the scream of the aircraft, the vicious thud and flash of guns, the sight of the falling bombs, a sweating gun-crew hoisting shells, slamming breeches and squeezing triggers without a word being spoken; men oblivious of everything and anything, including fear.

For these men, strung taut to the very limit of physical and mental tension, fear, anxiety and the near certainty of death – did not exist. That had been replaced by something far more important, the will to live and that could only be achieved by the intractable determination to kill. The Junkers, pulling up their noses at barely 300 feet into maximum climb, engines labouring in a snarling clamour, had each released their bombs to tumble down on target. A second later, with a tremendous roar they exploded in a blinding flash among the volatile cargo. The result was a huge rolling ball of flame as the ship blew up in a mushroom of fire and a giant column of billowing smoke.

Swept along her whole length by flames, the blast heeled *Waimarama* over to starboard, with petrol and ammunition blowing up in a series of booming reports. One Junker, close behind his leaders, lifting sharply to try to avoid the blast, was caught by the mass of fragments from the decks and superstructure and simply disintegrated in mid-air. And then, amid the flames, came a succession of dull, heavy explosions, rumbling across the sea, as her masts and part of the bridge structure, lurched, paused, then glowing red, slowly, ponderously, fell inwards into the melting furnace. Inside this floating crematorium, many were trapped within its iron wall. As *Waimarama* surrendered to the calm, flat sea, there came the dreadful sound of spluttering and hissing, as its hot hull sank deeper into the cold water. Within minutes she was gone, leaving the sea afire, burdened with tons of fuel oil, fashioning a carpet of twisting, licking flames.

That much Lieutenant-Commander Hill, following some distance behind in the little destroyer *Ledbury* could see, as he raced his ship forward. Then with heart-palpitating shock he saw something else, for within that burning sea were men, swimming, struggling men, not just a few but dozens, trapped and dying with the horrifying inevitability of death from drowning, burning or asphyxiation, for the flames of burning oil on water swallow up all oxygen on the surface. But there were also sounds, terrifying sounds, as men in an inherent instinct from self-preservation, in a fear-maddened frenzy, screamed their way to extinction.

Here and there, gouts of flame leaped from the surface in luminous incandescence to throw a picture which would for ever be burnt into the hearts and minds of those who watched. Human torches who thrashed insanely at the hungry flames before being released in the blessed oblivion of death.

Despite the danger, Hill moved in and lowered boats to recover those who remained alive. With rescue nets rigged along the ship's side, great acts of bravery were shown by two of *Ledbury*'s crew who went over the side again and again to bring men back to the ship. From the explosions and holocaust of fire that followed, it seemed impossible that anyone could have survived, yet out of *Waimarama*'s crew of 121, 32 were saved. The loss of 89 men in such tragic circumstances was a shattering blow to the morale of the crew of the remaining ships.

In his report the *Waimarama*'s Third Radio Officer John Jackson states that at the time the bombs struck, he was on the bridge talking to another officer. The explosions immediately enveloped the ship in flames to such an extent that he could not see the gun mountings only three yards away. Instinctively noting there was a patch of water clear of flames, he jumped overboard, only to remember that he could not swim. After the initial shock, he discovered he still had his life-jacket on, but he was walled in by flames and could not move away. At that point, seventeen-year-old cadet Treeves, on his first trip to sea, swam to him and towed him clear. Having found a piece of floating debris, he placed Jackson on it, then swam around to assist others. Two hours later, a whaler from *Ledbury* picked them up.

These two young men were the sole survivors of all the officers. Immediately astern of the blazing *Waimarama* and moving at fourteen knots came *Melbourne Star* and the tanker *Ohio*. The former's master, Captain MacFarlane, saw that his ship was heading straight for the inferno and, although the helm was put hard to port, there was no way to avoid the flaming sea. A ship of 13,000 tons does not respond immediately to helm movements. There is always a defined sideways or lateral motion, like the broadside skidding of a car, and the faster the speed and sharper the turn, the more violent the skid.

As a result, *Melbourne Star* steamed straight through the fires. That the ship did not blow up was a miracle, for she carried the same lethal cargo as *Waimarama*. In those fear-paralysing moments, the furnace of heat drove Captain Macfarlane into the shelter of the bridge. Expecting his ship to blow up at any moment, he shouted to the crew to go forward. The flames around them were now mast high, with the paint on the ship's side afire and the lifeboat's bottoms charred and burning. Large pieces of glowing hot debris were hurled aboard in the form of steel plates, pieces of ventilators and heavy angle irons, destroying the gun mountings. In a seeming eternity of time which could only have lasted seconds, *Melbourne Star* burst through the holocaust and came clear, leaving the blaze astern.

As the ship returned to normality, it was found that thirty-six men were missing. These, expecting the ship to blow up, had jumped over the side but found themselves in a worse situation among the flaming oil. Fortunately, the faithful *Ledbury* was there to pick them up. As Admiral Burrough said later of her, she was always at the right place at the right time.

Ohio, like *Melbourne Star* also found it impossible to avoid *Waimarama*'s cauldron of fire. It will be remembered from the earlier torpedo attack, that the hole in her side had allowed kerosene to spill from her tanks into the sea and this was still flowing as the tanker approached the flames. Once this ignited, the tanker would be doomed. With agonized desperation, Mason ordered 'Hard to port', but the tanker, slow to respond, moved closer and closer. In the nail-biting tension that followed, the crew counted the seconds, measured the distance, and slowly, so very slowly, *Ohio* swung away, just clearing the edge of the burning sea.

Half an hour later, another attack developed from a group of the dreaded Stuka dive-bombers, accompanied by Italian fighters. During this determined and accurate raid, *Ohio* was selected for attention and, within minutes, Mason found himself in a battle for survival. Peeling off to attack, the Stukas roared down, pulling out of their dives from just above mast height, the strange shape of their dihedral wings clearly identifying themselves. Apart from its shape, the principal and positive identification of the Stuka is the fearsome noise of its dive created by an aerodynamic device fitted to the wings. This produces an ear-splitting scream intended to put the fear of God into the targeted victims before the bombs are released.

The importance of the one tanker surviving to reach Malta was vigorously emphasized by the guns that had been installed on *Ohio*. These were manned by twelve army and seven naval gunners. Every gun on the tanker opened up, swivelling from high angle to low angle, sweeping to meet the cunning diversity of attack. This was war, bitter war, a face-to-face confrontation, with the ship's gunners blasting shells into the cockpits of enemy aircraft only a few hundred feet away, and the German pilots trying to flight their bombs to extinguish all resistance. The deck gunners, smoke-grimed, half-choked with cordite fumes, wiped the sweat from their eyes and, like automatons programmed to perform, loaded and fired, loaded and fired. They had no hatred of the enemy. Knowledge is the forerunner of hatred and they had no personal knowledge of the men who were trying to kill them. However reluctant the combatants may be, in the heat of confrontation options are non-existent. There is one law only, kill or be killed.

There were certainly no slackers among the gunners. Every man did his job with all the strength and ability he could muster. He had to, for each fought for his own survival and for the survival of the ship which kept him afloat. The author, from his own experience can testify that there is nothing so terrifying as being on the deck of a ship with Stuka bombers diving at you in a near vertical angle at 400 miles per hour, listening to its ear-piercing screaming whistle and watching the fall of its bombs tumbling directly towards you, before it pulls out of its dive, seemingly just above mast height.

The concentrated fire from *Ohio*'s unflinching gunners

brought its results, with the two leading Stukas clawed out of the sky, bursting into flame before hitting the sea. A third, changing his tactics, levelled off some distance away, and came in on a firing track. Too low, he brushed against the sea, glanced off, bounced crazily in a series of hops and then with his wing-tip hitting the water, somersaulted to collide against the starboard hull and descended on to the foredeck with a tremendous crash. That its bombs failed to explode was nothing short of a miracle, for, if they had done so, it would have wiped out the forward gun's crew. Unknown to Mason, who had his hands full trying to avoid the fall of bombs from diving planes, another aircraft was hit by the after-gunners with similar result, landing on the ship's after-deck. Moments later, the chief officer telephoned from aft in great excitement to say that a Stuka bomber had landed on the poop deck. Mason, who had been on the bridge all night and without sleep for many hours, replied, 'Oh, that's nothing, we've had a Stuka on the foredeck for nearly half-an-hour.'

With other enemy planes arriving to supplement the raid, the bombing became continuous, and it was only the accuracy of fire from the gunners that saved the ship from a direct hit. One near miss, however, right under the bows, opened up the starboard and port bow tanks, buckled the plating and flooded the forward tank. Other hazards appeared in the form of bunches of parachutes being dropped in front of the convoy each with a mine attached and measuring some three feet across. Only by executing various emergency turns were these avoided.

At 10.30 a.m. that day, a concentrated attack by Italian torpedo bombers developed, which was given a reception of withering gunfire. This broke up the formation so effectively that, in their efforts to avoid destruction, the pilots dropped their torpedoes in all directions, anywhere but in line with the convoy. The Commodore's ship *Port Chalmers*, which thus far had borne a charmed life amid innumerable bombs and torpedoes, had an incredible escape. One torpedo passed directly under her keel, while another careered past the hull on her starboard side. Minutes later, her paravane wire began to vibrate violently. (A paravane is a fish-shaped device, with fins or vanes, towed from the bow, for deflecting mines along a wire and severing their moorings.) With the ship stopped, the paravane itself was slowly hauled out of water, revealing a live torpedo hanging by its fin, with the deadly warhead swaying dangerously close to the side of the ship. In the next few nail-biting moments, it was lowered gently back into the sea and the paravane wire cut while *Port Chalmers* hastily drew astern.

Seconds later, as the torpedo hit the seabed, it exploded with such force, it lifted the ship bodily. But by now *Dorset* was in trouble, near-missed by six bombs which had started a fire near the storage of petrol and flooded the engine-room to put it out of action. With no hope of saving her, the order 'Abandon ship' was given, and the crew were picked up by the destroyer *Bramham* which was already crammed with survivors from other ships.

Out of the original fourteen freighters with their precious cargoes, only four now remained with their escorts, *Port Chalmers, Melbourne Star* and *Rochester Castle*, all damaged but still afloat and moving under their own power, with the crippled tanker *Ohio* far to the rear with *Penn* in attendance. By mid-afternoon, the leading three merchant ships were within sight of the island with the short-range Spitfires keeping the bombers at a distance, and by five o'clock that afternoon, to the frenzied cheers of the crowds of Maltese who had gathered at the shores to greet them, the three freighters, battered and broken, their flame-blistered hulls bearing evidence of the torment of the last three days, moved slowly between the welcoming arms of the breakwater at Valetta. Later that day, the fifth surviving ship *Brisbane Star*, who with her crumpled bows had successfully made her lone voyage along the Tunisian coast, also arrived. But the *Rochester Castle*, with 4,000 tons of water flooding her holds and her gunwales only six feet above water, just managed to berth before settling her keel on the seabed in the shallow water of the harbour.

Although Malta now had food to break the siege, albeit temporarily, its position was still precarious. Without *Ohio*'s oil, the island could not survive and that cargo was still eighty miles away to the west. It was on this ship, the barely moving *Ohio*, that the fate of Malta mainly depended. Alone, except for *Penn*, *Ohio* became the sole target for more bomber strikes. At ten o'clock the following morning, a force of heavy bombers dived low over the ship and dropped a cluster of bombs shaving down each side.

Under this impact, *Ohio* was lifted out of the water, shaking violently from stem to stern. Minutes later the main engines stopped as water flooded into the engine-room, and then one of the boilers blew out to extinguish the fires. All this time, the bombers were roaring in, trying to finish the stationary target, and it was only the accurate barrage by the gunners that thwarted their endeavours to come closer. By a wonder-working effort from the engineers, engines were re-started allowing the ship to move forward but at only four knots.

At this point the destroyer *Ledbury* came alongside offering a tow, and it was estimated that together they could make twelve knots. Thirty minutes later, however, the second boiler blew out, extinguishing the remaining fires and leaving the vessel again stopped. *Ledbury* then received orders from Admiral Burrough that she should speed west to pick up survivors from the sunken cruiser *Manchester*, which left only *Penn* to assist. As the destroyer carefully came alongside, a party of *Ohio*'s crew set to work to clear away the fuselage of the crashed German aircraft off the foredeck. Even while this was in progress, the crew was forced to throw themselves flat as more bombs came hurtling down. Eventually, when all was made ready, *Penn* began to tow.

Ohio was a dead weight. Each time the destroyer took up the strain it brought the tanker yawing to port. Mason watched anxiously as the tow whipped out of the water, hurling a shower of spray as it pulled momentarily taut and then plunged back into the sea, while *Penn* responded sluggishly to the heave. Each time it lifted to bar tautness, quivering under the strain, it seemed as though it might be the last.

Ohio, stubbornly resisting the haul, seemed to be protesting, with the strident noise of creaking and jarring from the tortured metal of her torn plates. Minutes later, the tow, unequal to the excessive demands made upon it, snapped with a report like that of a pistol shot. The rope, like an uncoiled spring, lashed back to whip across the forecastle deck to tangle itself around bollards and stanchions.

Mason realized that the only hope for his ship was to have two destroyers, one towing and one astern to act as a rudder. It was certainly an idea worth trying but there was no second destroyer. In any case, despite their indomitable courage in the face of such adversity, the crew's physical and mental effectiveness had been stretched to danger level. There is only so much a man can take, a limit to which human endurance can be stretched and the men of *Ohio* had reached that limit. Mason himself, was rocking on his feet with exhaustion, racked with the torture of self-discipline not to allow himself to weaken. He, like his men, had been without sleep for what seemed like an eternity. Sleep starvation is one thing but sleep starvation compounded by almost every moment poised within an ace of death, is entirely different. The body's demand for adrenalin has its limitations. And it was at this point, with the ship almost within sight of Malta, that that physical and mental threshhold had been reached.

It was hell enough for the crew but at least in the very brief spell between one bombing attack and another, between one torpedo strike and another, between the savage machine-gunning of the decks and another, they could droop themselves over guns or stanchions or prop themselves up against a piece of superstructure for a few moments to ease their burning eyes and pretend to be awake. Mason, however, could not. He was the captain, and the ship was his responsibility. There were always emergencies, on the decks, at the guns, below in the engine-room or on the bridge, signals to be sent or signals to be received and understood and acted upon. The ship and the crew depended upon him.

When bombs are tumbling towards the ship, when torpedoes are skidding past the hulls, the laws of the sea, the rules of the road, all so carefully and explicitly defined in the *Seamanship Manual*, no longer apply. To survive, you make the rules as you go along. Mason was there all the time, driving, encouraging, holding everything and everybody together by sheer determination and personality; his presence was absolutely essential, he had to stay awake.

With *Ohio* now stationary, powerless to move, unable to be towed and still subject to constant bombing, the one thought in Mason's mind was to save his crew. He therefore requested *Penn* to take off his men until further assistance became available, and at two o'clock that afternoon the destroyer took aboard the whole crew. There was nothing further that Mason could do and he followed them reluctantly, wondering if this was to be the end of the vessel which he and his crew had fought so hard to save.

The tanker, alone, deserted, presented a pathetic picture, low in the water, blasted, battered and scarred. The entire upperworks, fore and aft, were a twisted jungle of broken steel, while the smoke stack presented nothing less than a shrapnel-punctured, jagged vertical cylinder. The remnants of the Stuka lay across the forecastle, the skeleton of another athwart the poop-deck. Here and there, plumes of smoke, licked by little tongues of flame, persisted in breaking out along the main deck which was already split across. Aboard *Penn*, the men of *Ohio* found odd corners and dropped into instant sleep, a deep sleep from which no amount of banging or clanging would awaken them.

Magnificent *Ohio*

While Mason and his crew slept the sleep of exhaustion, *Penn* circled the drifting tanker, awaiting assistance either from another destroyer or a tug from Malta. During the next four hours, more strong attacks developed with dive bombers and torpedo bombers, later to be supplemented by Italian aircraft. Altogether nearly seventy aircraft were employed in these raids. However, the effect of these attacks was somewhat mitigated by the presence of the Royal Air Force, maintaining an umbrella of Spitfires above the tanker.

Despite this, several aircraft managed to penetrate the screen and bomb the ship. Just before six o'clock that evening, two motor launches and the minesweeper *Rye* arrived from Malta. Mason, now a little refreshed, called for volunteers from his crew to go back on *Ohio* to make the tow fast. Despite the existing bombing and with only three hours sleep, the whole crew voluntarily returned.

They were not compelled to do so, not constrained to go back to face the possibility of being killed, with the enemy's venom targeted on the tanker. They were far safer on *Penn*. Once again this new crisis, this new challenge was to be met and contained, and somehow, they found an endurance within themselves they had no idea existed. Few of them had any thoughts that what they were doing was for King and Country. That was a carefully cherished myth, propagated by the gallant leaders of the popular press, who, to sell their newspapers, churned out volumes of patriotic claptrap. For the men of *Ohio*, the last border of hope and endurance was not patriotism but the fundamental and basic emotions of pity for the people of Malta and, something they had all learned in the last few days, comradeship between and for one another.

And there was something else; a stubborn, bloody-minded pigheadedness to see this thing through to the bitter end. In this short time, the men and the ship had become part of one another. Mortally wounded though *Ohio* might be, the crew were damned if they were going to let her grave be the deep waters of the Mediterranean. If she had to meet her end, it would be within the safe waters of Valetta harbour.

As they swarmed aboard, the tows were made fast to *Penn* and *Rye* and with both ships going slowly ahead, a four-to-five knot progress was maintained. Half an hour later, the ominous sounds of another air attack were heard.

This time the raid was launched from astern, a direction in which the guns of *Ohio* and the two naval vessels found it difficult to bring their defences to bear. The approach was perfect, four Junker 88s, dead on the centre line, with the first bomb landing close astern, smashing the rudder, the second, an armour-piercing bomb slicing contemptuously through the boat-deck plating, through into the engine-room to explode on top of the boilers, starting a fire. Hundreds of tons of water rushed in, smashing through cross-bulkheads fractured by the explosion and ripping open watertight doors buckled by the blast. Within seconds came the roar of escaping steam and the resounding crash of massive boilers being torn from their stools.

Ohio should have died then; nothing built by man could have been expected to withstand such an assault. She should have gone under or turned over or been blown apart. But she did none of these things. By a miracle she held together and that she did not die can only be attributed to the professional skills of her American builders. Incredibly, she was holding together by the strength of her keel. There had unfortunately been one casualty, a gunner, who later died from internal injuries. During this raid, *Penn* and *Rye* were also near-missed and were forced to cast off the tow. *Ohio* was now so low that her tanker deck was just above water. As Mason saw no point in remaining on board, with the consequent risk to life when stopped from continuous air attacks, he ordered the crew to the boats divided between the motor-launches and the destroyers. Although it seemed to Mason that the chances of saving his ship were fading, inwardly he was determined to make every effort given at least a fair chance.

With the coming of night giving blessed relief from air attack, Mason boarded one of the launches and managed to gain a few hours sleep to face whatever the morrow might bring. That evening the destroyer *Bramham* arrived to join the fight to save *Ohio*. While Mason and his crew collapsed into a sleep of exhaustion, the destroyer captains discussed ways and means of trying to tow the unwieldy weight.

With the first lightening of the eastern sky, tired men willingly, resolutely, dragged themselves back to their stations. There was an unyielding determination to succeed. Behind them were the memories, the tensions, the accumulative physics of exhaustion; before them the hopes, the ambitions, the yearning to gain their objective. But hardly had they settled to their tasks when once again came the familiar drone of aircraft. Surely now, so close to Malta, they could be spared further bombing ordeals. The bombers and fighters, however, swept in, trying to fight their way through the defence umbrella of Spitfires and Beaufighters. Some succeeded in penetrating the defences, and soon bombs were falling all around the drifting tanker.

Mason, in one of the motor-launches approaching *Ohio* was then to witness what he thought at the time was the death of his ship. A 1,000-lb bomb, falling within a few feet of the stern, carried away the whole rudder structure and blew a great hole in the after part. It seemed to him that she must surely succumb to this latest attack. But as the tall column of water fell back into the sea and the smoke cleared he saw to his amazement she still floated.

Certainly she had settled by the stern and, from the groans of tortured metal amidships, he knew that her back was broken but she was still there and holding. And at that moment, further help appeared with the arrival of the minesweeper *Speedy*, three more motor-launches and the destroyer *Ledbury*. When Mason climbed aboard *Ohio*, he made a thorough examination of the ship and found that, among other damage, kerosene was pouring out fast from the port tanks and water flooding in through the holed side and stern. Furthermore, there was a distinct possibility that she could break in half at any time, in which case the stern half would probably fall off, leaving the forward section which contained 75 per cent of her oil cargo to be towed and hopefully reach the island. Frustrated in this attack, which proved to be the last attempt to sink the tanker, the planes flew off, droning their way back to base in Sicily.

Despite all the failures in the past few hours to get the tanker moving, and the frequent parting of the tows, another concerted effort was made to save the ship. *Rye* moved in to the bows and passed a cable to the working party on the forecastle, while *Ledbury* secured a wire to the stern to act as a rudder. *Penn* and *Bramham* then closed in and secured themselves to the ship, one on each side, to hold *Ohio* up. Gradually, with the towing ships going slow ahead, *Ohio* began to move again at five knots. At this agonizingly slow pace, the little cluster of ships moved towards Malta with the water-level in the flooded engine-room growing deeper with every mile gained. During these last few tortuous miles and when within sight of the island, *Bramham*'s tow parted yet again. Were they to be denied the victory almost within their grasp?

With a new tow secured, *Ohio* again set off, almost crawling towards her goal. As the last of the 'Pedestal' operation drew to its breathless close, the deliverance of Malta from humiliating surrendering rested on this one ship, *Ohio*, fabulous, famous, magnificent, ever to be remembered. A strange and stricken sight, with shattered superstructure, crazily tilted, gaping holes exuding oil and kerosene, she still presented a ghostly epitaph of endurance. On either side of the bows, along the hull, before the bridge and in a score of places, huge patches of crimson and black showed through, where missed bombs and flames had stripped off the paint.

Ohio's survival depended as much on her construction as on the strength, perseverance and courage of Captain Mason and his crew, to bring the tanker into the Grand Harbour to discharge her precariously preserved cargo. By eight o'clock on the morning of 15 August 1942, by magnificent seamanship on the part of the destroyers, *Ohio* was slowly and tenderly manoeuvred into position alongside another berthed tanker and lashed to its hull. There at the quayside, a fantastic welcome from waving, cheering crowds, seemingly the entire population, greeted the arrival of the tanker whose name would resound throughout Malta's long history for many, many years.

But the cheering and the waving was not reserved only for *Ohio*, but also for the crews of the few faithful destroyers and minesweepers which had resuscitated *Ohio* and ushered her in the last few miles, the last few yards. Within minutes, Maltese dockyard men swarmed aboard the tanker and, by the attachment of pipes and pumps, began to unload her precious cargo.

Even as the last few gallons left the tanks, *Ohio* settled her keel gently on to the seabed. She had done her duty and served her purpose, far beyond anything her builders could have expected of her. *Ohio* had indeed carved her name in maritime history. The gallant master of *Ohio*, Captain Dudley Mason, lost no time in paying tribute to his officers and crew with many commendations. Following the events described, he received the award of the George Cross in salvaging his ship at a time when her untimely end seemed inevitable.

The citation read:

> His Majesty the King has been pleased to award the George Cross to Captain D.W. Mason in recognition of the gallantry displayed by him and his crew, as a result of which, the major part of *Ohio*'s cargo, so vital to the defence of Malta, reached its destination.
>
> *London Gazette*
> *8 September 1942*

The Prime Minister Winston Churchill aptly summed it up in *The Second World War*:

> Thus in the end, five gallant merchant ships out of fourteen got through with their precious cargoes. The loss of three hundred and fifty officers and men and of so many fine ships of the Merchant Navy and in the escorting fleet of the Royal Navy was grievous. The reward justified the price exacted. Revictualled and replenished with ammunition and vital stores, the strength of Malta revived. British submarines returned to the island, and, with the striking forces of the Royal Air Force, regained their dominating position in the Central Mediterranean. It should have been within the enemy's power, as it was clearly his interest to destroy this convoy utterly.

Malta had been saved but at what a price. Although 'Pedestal' had not entirely raised the siege, it increased the Maltese people's rations a little, raised morale and gave new hope for survival. Among the cargo which had arrived, there was oil and aviation spirit to serve the Spitfires and Beaufighters and the submarines, and ammunition for the fighting armed services in defence of the island. Gradually the intensity of the raids on Malta diminished, and in November the siege was finally raised when a convoy arrived from Alexandria with stocks of food, ammunition and fuel. By December, food was arriving in plenty, with a welcome Christmas present of a cargo of 77,000 tons.

The story of the ships of the Malta convoy has a special place in the pages of maritime history, which will be read by millions of people who are stirred by tales of high endeavour and supreme sacrifice. The fortitude and valour of the men of the merchant navy, in facing up to what was probably the most dangerous voyage of World War II, is doubly advanced by the fact that they were not trained for war like their Royal Navy colleagues. And yet because of their courage, determination and heroism, and despite the terrible losses sustained in that endeavour, Malta and its people were saved.

Bibliography

Books
Campbell, C., *The World War II Fact Book* (Macdonald, 1985)
Campbell, Ian, *The Kola Run* (Futura, 1975)
Churchill, Winston S., *The Second World War* (Cassell, 1949)
Humble, Richard, *Hitler's High Seas Fleet* (Pan/Ballantine, 1972)
Lund, Paul & Ludlam, Harry, *PQ17: Convoy to Hell* (New English Library, 1973)
Robertson, Terence, *Walker RN* (Evans, 1956)
Schofield, Brian, *The Russian Convoys* (Batsford, 1964; Pan, 1971)
Shankland, Peter & Hunter, Anthony, *Malta Convoy* (Fontana, 1961)
Smith, Ure, *Encyclopedia of Sea Warfare* (Salamander, 1975)
Taylor, J.C., *German Warships of World War II* (Ian Allan, 1966)

Journal
Review Journal, Naval Historical Collectors' and Research Association

Index

189